PERFECTLY CREAMY

FROZEN YOGURT

PERFECTLY CREAMY
FROZEN YOGURT

56 AMAZING FLAVORS
plus Recipes for Pies, Cakes
& Other Frozen Desserts

NICOLE WESTON

PHOTOGRAPHY BY
Matt Armendariz

Storey Publishing

The mission of Storey Publishing is to serve our customers by publishing practical information that encourages personal independence in harmony with the environment.

Edited by Sarah Guare

Art direction and book design by Jeff Stiefel

Text production by Erin Dawson

Indexed by Christine R. Lindemer, Boston Road Communications

Cover and interior photography by © Matt Armendariz, except pages 7, 15 (right), and 74 by Mars Vilaubi

Storey Publishing
210 MASS MoCA Way
North Adams, MA 01247
storey.com

Printed in China by Toppan Leefung Printing Ltd.
10 9 8 7 6 5 4 3 2 1

Library of Congress Cataloging-in-Publication Data
Names: Weston, Nicole, author.
Title: Perfectly creamy frozen yogurt : 56 amazing flavors plus recipes for pies, cakes & other frozen desserts / Nicole Weston.
Description: North Adams, MA : Storey Publishing, [2018] | Includes bibliographical references and index.
Identifiers: LCCN 2017050486 (print) | LCCN 2017046697 (ebook) | ISBN 9781612128801 (pbk. : alk. paper) | ISBN 9781612128818 (ebook)
Subjects: LCSH: Frozen yogurt. | Cooking (Yogurt) | LCGFT: Cookbooks.
Classification: LCC TX795 .W486 2018 (ebook) | LCC TX795 (print) | DDC 641.6/71476—dc23
LC record available at https://lccn.loc.gov/2017050486

To Mom, Dad, and Rob,
for all their support and willingness
to eat as much frozen yogurt
as I could make

CONTENTS

8 **How to Make Creamy, Slightly Tangy, Pure Frozen Yogurt**

CREAMY, SLIGHTLY TANGY, PURE

FROZEN YOGURT

As a kid on hot days in Southern California, I always looked forward to enjoying a cool treat after a long day at school. Sometimes I had an ice-cold soda or a smoothie, but the treat I loved most was frozen yogurt.

When frozen yogurt first became popular, it was as a soft-serve substitute for ice cream. It was sweet and creamy, but it came in very few identifiable flavors and its main selling point was that it was a lower-fat, more healthful alternative to traditional ice cream. It was hugely popular when it became available in the early 1980s, but growth in the frozen yogurt market slowed after a few years because the yogurt itself was bland and more compelling as a vehicle for toppings like shredded coconut, yogurt chips, and rainbow sprinkles than as a unique treat.

Plain yogurt has a tart, tangy flavor that comes from the natural cultures that are used to turn ordinary milk into what we know as yogurt. Yogurt wasn't very popular when frozen yogurt was first introduced, except among the very health conscious, but as better-tasting, thicker yogurts grew in popularity, frozen yogurt also started to change — and to taste like yogurt. That signature yogurt tang became a hallmark of high-quality frozen yogurts made with premium ingredients. This new style of frozen yogurt launched a yogurt revolution, and it is now more popular than ever before.

The recipes that follow show you how to make frozen desserts at home with the tangy, fresh flavor of premium frozen yogurts.

METHOD AND EQUIPMENT

Frozen yogurt is a dessert made with yogurt as its base, but there is a big difference between yogurt that has been frozen and frozen yogurt. Yogurt that has been frozen is grainy and icy. It shatters instead of scoops and does not blend well with added ingredients.

Frozen yogurt should be creamy and smooth, and — like ice cream — it should be something that you can store in your freezer and scoop when you want to eat some. It's easy to make at home, and making your own frozen yogurt gives you complete control of the ingredients and flavors that will go into your desserts.

Frozen yogurt does present some challenges that ice cream does not.

Yogurt doesn't freeze well on its own because a major component of yogurt is whey, the watery part of milk. Whey freezes solid, just like water. So when you freeze plain yogurt, it develops icy crystals and loses its texture — and the same thing can happen to homemade frozen yogurt. You end up with something that's a far cry from the creamy, smooth texture that you want in a frozen dessert.

Commercially made frozen yogurts often have stabilizers added to enhance their texture, and commercial machines can infuse enough extra air into the base to keep the frozen yogurt soft. Home ice cream makers aren't as powerful as commercial machines, but there are a few things you can do to ensure that your frozen yogurt tastes delicious and stays scoopable even after sitting in the freezer for a few days.

The first trick is to minimize the amount of whey in your frozen yogurt base by using thick, Greek-style yogurt, which already has a lot of the whey strained out of it. This thicker yogurt will be less likely to form large ice crystals when frozen. The second trick is to use full-fat yogurt and dairy, since the little bit of extra fat will give your frozen yogurt additional creaminess. The small amount of fat will also help prevent the yogurt from freezing too hard. Finally, the most important thing you can do to achieve a pleasing, scoopable texture is to infuse extra air into your yogurt mixture before churning. I call this the Meringue Method, because I use an easy-to-make meringue to aerate the base and help ensure a deliciously smooth finished product every time.

The Meringue Method

The Meringue Method for making frozen yogurt involves using a cooked meringue, also known as an Italian meringue, to incorporate extra air into the frozen yogurt base before the churning phase. Meringue is a mixture of egg whites and sugar that is beaten until stiff and foamy. Most meringues are made with raw eggs and then incorporated into recipes that call for cooking the meringue before serving. The Italian meringue uses a different technique to produce meringue that is completely cooked and safe to eat without any additional cooking or baking; it is an ideal addition to frozen yogurt. The meringue is very easy to prepare and makes a big difference in the creaminess of the finished yogurt.

To make a cooked meringue, you first beat room-temperature egg whites until they're foamy. Then you slowly stream boiling sugar into the egg whites while beating them until soft peaks form. The egg whites in the finished meringue are completely cooked; you can fold them into any yogurt mixture without additional cooking.

Another advantage of the Meringue Method is that the melted sweetener for the recipe is easily incorporated into the yogurt. Many recipes call for long periods of strong stirring to dissolve granulated sugar into the yogurt. So, though it may seem complicated at first, it takes only a few minutes to make the meringue, and the results are well worth the effort.

Making Frozen Yogurt with an Ice Cream Maker

Most of the recipes in this book call for using an ice cream maker to churn your frozen yogurt base into actual frozen yogurt. There is a wide variety of ice cream makers on the market. They come in many sizes and in a range of prices, so you are sure to find something that will suit your needs. An ice cream maker will give you the best results and allow you to make frozen yogurt much more quickly than doing it by hand.

The purpose of an ice cream maker is to chill an ice cream or frozen yogurt base mixture quickly while adding air to it. Rapid chilling reduces the number and size of ice crystals in the finished product, so it will be smooth and creamy. Adding air to the mixture softens it, making it easy to scoop when frozen. That added air also makes frozen desserts taste better, since slight aeration allows the frozen mixture to melt smoothly and evenly on your tongue.

Making Frozen Yogurt without an Ice Cream Maker

Ice cream makers turn the process of creating frozen yogurt into a job that's quick and easy, but it is possible to make frozen yogurt without an ice cream maker. To do this, simply make the yogurt base of your choice and pour it into a large baking dish. Place the baking dish in the freezer and come back and give the mixture a thorough stir with a fork after 15 to 20 minutes. This breaks up any large ice crystals that may have formed during the freezing. Check back every 15 to 20 minutes, repeating the stirring process until the base has become thick and is mostly frozen. At this point, you can stir in any flavorings the recipe calls for and then serve your frozen yogurt or transfer it to another container for longer storage.

Frozen yogurt made without an ice cream maker will still have great flavor, but it may have some chunks of ice in it that batches made in an ice cream maker won't have. It might also freeze harder if you store it long-term and require some extra thawing time before you can scoop and serve it.

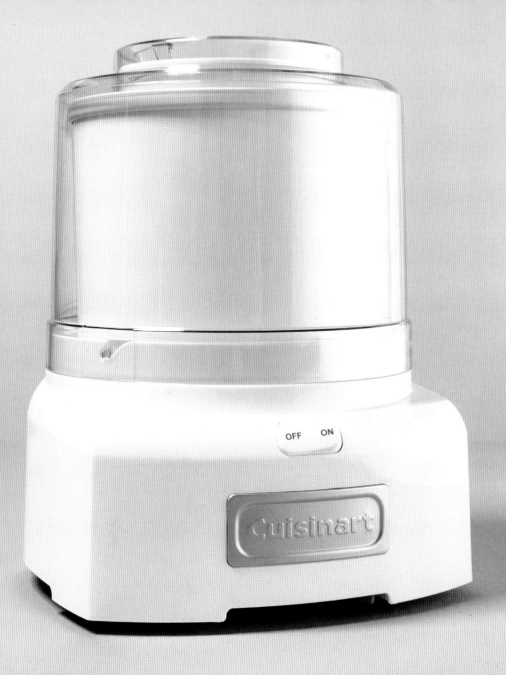

THE CANISTER ICE CREAM MAKER is the most common type. This model has a thick-walled canister: you freeze it in advance, and then you simply pour your base into the frozen canister and churn away. Some canister models require you to hand-churn your ice cream or frozen yogurt, but most are small electric appliances that will do the work for you. Some stand mixers even offer canister attachments that will temporarily turn the mixer into an ice cream maker. The only drawback with this appliance is that you have to do some advance planning, making sure to put the canister in the freezer about 24 hours before you want to make your frozen yogurt.

THE HAND-CHURN ICE CREAM MAKER is the most basic kind. With this type of gadget, you add your own ice and salt to one chamber and your ice cream or frozen yogurt base to the other, and then you shake or stir while the base thickens up. This maker is very inexpensive and produces softer ice creams, but it works and it gives you a real workout as you churn up each batch.

THE COMPRESSOR ICE CREAM MAKER is the most expensive type. The internal compressor starts to freeze your base as soon as you turn the appliance on. You don't have to prefreeze anything, and you don't even need to chill your dessert base before adding it to the machine, although doing so speeds up the freezing process. The advantage of this type of ice cream maker is that the machine is always ready to go and is capable of making multiple batches, one right after another, with no waiting time. This sort of pricey machine may not suit the occasional ice cream maker, but if you love to make ice cream or find that you are often serving a crowd, you can get a lot of use out of one of these.

STEP-BY-STEP FROZEN YOGURT

1 Combine water and sugar in a small saucepan. Bring to a boil and boil for 1 minute.

2 Beat egg whites to soft peaks in a large bowl.

3 Remove the boiling sugar from the heat and slowly stream into the egg whites with the mixer running.

4 Beat to a glossy, finished meringue, 2 to 3 minutes.

5 Combine the yogurt and flavoring ingredients in a large bowl and whisk until smooth.

6 Fold the meringue into the yogurt mixture.

7 Pour the yogurt mixture into an ice cream maker and churn according to the manufacturer's directions.

8 If adding mix-ins, transfer the churned yogurt to a large bowl and stir in additions.

9 Transfer the yogurt to a freezer-safe container and chill in the freezer for 2 to 3 hours. Then, eat!

MIX-INS

You can customize your frozen yogurt by adding a wide variety of mix-ins to any recipe just after churning. Chopped cookies, toasted nuts, shredded coconut, chocolate chunks, and fresh berries are just some of the many tasty additions you might already have on hand. Get creative!

START FROM SCRATCH BY MAKING YOUR OWN YOGURT

Great frozen yogurt starts with delicious yogurt, so you should always choose a brand that has a flavor you like. Alternatively, you can make your own yogurt and use it as a base for your frozen yogurt creations.

Yogurt is easy to make at home, and yogurt fans might find that they like their homemade version better than anything available at the grocery store. You need to start with some bacteria to get the yogurt process going. You can either purchase yogurt cultures from a specialty catalog or use a small amount of a favorite brand of yogurt that contains live, active *Lactobacillus acidophilus* cultures, the bacteria that turn milk into yogurt. If you are going to use store-bought yogurt as a starter, read the label carefully to ensure that it contains live cultures, or your homemade yogurt will not thicken up properly. The best yogurts to use will have very short ingredient lists and will not include stabilizers or thickeners, such as gelatin or cornstarch. Once you have made a batch of your own yogurt, you can reserve a small portion of it to act as a starter for your next batch.

Yogurt cultures are temperature sensitive, so you will want to use an instant-read thermometer when you're making yogurt. You may also want to invest in a yogurt maker, which makes the process just about foolproof and also allows you to easily portion your yogurt into small containers for serving. If you decide you want to make your own yogurt on a regular basis, a yogurt maker is a great investment that will repay you for a long time to come.

Nevertheless, even without a yogurt maker, you can make yogurt at home — you'll just need to keep a closer eye on your mixture as it develops to make sure it stays in a good temperature range for the cultures.

PLAIN YOGURT

4 cups (1 quart) whole milk

¼ cup plain yogurt with live, active yogurt cultures, room temperature

1 Bring the milk to a simmer in a large saucepan.

2 Remove the pan from the heat just before the milk boils. Cool the milk to 110°F/43°C, using a thermometer to check the temperature.

3 Place the yogurt in a small bowl. When the milk has cooled to 110°F/43°C, add about 1 cup of the milk to the yogurt and whisk until the yogurt is completely incorporated. Pour the yogurt mixture into the milk and whisk to combine.

IF USING A YOGURT MAKER: Divide the milk mixture into the containers of your yogurt maker and process according to the manufacturer's directions. Refrigerate the yogurt after processing.

IF NOT USING A YOGURT MAKER: Transfer the milk mixture to a large clean jar or container with an airtight lid and close the lid tightly.

Place the jar in a very warm place and allow the yogurt to thicken undisturbed for about 10 hours. Ideally, the jar should be maintained at 110°F to 115°F/43°C to 46°C as the yogurt thickens. High shelves in warm rooms are good locations, and you can also create a warm environment for your yogurt by setting your oven to "warm." Check your warm place with a thermometer to see that it is in the right temperature range before you place your jar there. If you're using your oven, you may find when you do your temperature check that cracking the door slightly results in the right temperature range.

Makes about 4 cups

GREEK-STYLE YOGURT

4 cups (1 quart) plain yogurt

Greek-style yogurt can easily be made at home by straining some of the excess whey from a batch of plain yogurt. You can strain store-bought plain yogurt or homemade yogurt, and both will give you a wonderfully thick product to serve as the base of your frozen yogurts. You can use whole-milk, low-fat, or nonfat yogurt for this process. Different brands have different consistencies, so the draining time may vary slightly from batch to batch. Choose a high-quality yogurt that doesn't have additives or stabilizers in it.

You will need a very fine strainer to drain the whey without losing any of the yogurt. A strainer lined with cheesecloth is ideal because you can handle any quantity of yogurt, but the coffee filters that fit in your home coffeemaker (2- to 6-cup size) work well if you don't mind working in batches. You can use a very fine unlined strainer if you don't have either cheesecloth or coffee filters on hand.

1 Line a large strainer with two layers of cheesecloth, making sure that some of the cloth hangs over the sides of the strainer.

2 Place the strainer over a large bowl and fill with the yogurt. Cover the yogurt with extra cheesecloth and squeeze gently. Allow to sit for 1 to 2 hours at room temperature or up to 12 hours in the refrigerator. Excess whey will drain into the bowl.

3 When the yogurt remaining in the strainer is thick and creamy, transfer it to another container for storage in the refrigerator or use in frozen yogurt recipes. Discard the excess whey or save it for another use.

Makes about 3 cups

WHAT IS GREEK-STYLE YOGURT?

Greek-style yogurt is plain yogurt that has been strained to remove excess whey, resulting in a yogurt that is much thicker and creamier in consistency than ordinary yogurt. Authentic Greek-style yogurt does not get its texture from the addition of gelatin or stabilizers. Greek-style yogurt is available in many flavors, but the distinctive tangy flavor of plain is best for making flavorful frozen yogurt.

You can easily turn ordinary yogurt into Greek-style yogurt by straining it through cheesecloth or a very fine sieve for a few hours to remove most of the whey.

DO I NEED TO USE GREEK-STYLE YOGURT?

The excess whey — the watery part of milk — that is in regular yogurt will turn to ice when you use it in frozen yogurt. The frozen yogurt will still taste good straight out of the ice cream maker, but it will be a harder and icier frozen yogurt than one made with Greek-style yogurt.

WHAT BRAND OF YOGURT SHOULD I USE?

You can use any brand of yogurt; choose one that you like. You can even use homemade yogurt. Since you'll be adding flavorings and sweeteners, you should choose plain yogurt, not flavored yogurt, for these recipes.

CAN I USE NONFAT OR LOW-FAT YOGURT?

Yes, both nonfat and low-fat yogurt will turn out very tasty frozen yogurts and can be used in any of the recipes in this book. Full-fat yogurt will produce a creamier, richer-tasting product, which is why I recommend it for most frozen yogurts.

CAN I REDUCE THE SUGAR?

You can reduce the sugar, but your results will not be the same as with the original recipe. The frozen yogurt may be too hard and icy or may taste too tart if you reduce the sugar. Sugar has two important functions in frozen yogurt recipes: it helps the frozen yogurt remain creamy and smooth, rather than icy, and it also ensures just the right amount of sweetness in the finished dessert. The base for frozen yogurt will taste sweeter before it has been frozen, and you may find that your finished product is not sweet enough if you reduce the sugar in the initial recipe, even though the unfrozen base seems sweet.

DOES THE MERINGUE METHOD REALLY COOK THE EGG WHITES?

Yes, the boiling sugar is hot enough to cook the egg whites and make them completely safe to eat.

CAN I USE PROCESSED EGG WHITES INSTEAD OF WHITES FROM SEPARATED EGGS?

Processed egg whites are not ideal for making meringues. Though these egg whites are convenient, the pasteurization process toughens some of the proteins in the eggs and prevents the whites from whipping up into fluffy meringues. It could take up to twice as long to beat processed egg whites to soft peaks, and they won't be as fluffy as fresh egg whites will be.

DO I NEED AN ICE CREAM MAKER?

I've included instructions for making frozen yogurt without an ice cream maker, but you will generally get better results using an ice cream maker. An ice cream maker speeds up the freezing process and reduces the number of large ice crystals, resulting in a creamier finished product.

CAN I EAT MY FROZEN YOGURT STRAIGHT OUT OF THE ICE CREAM MAKER?

Yes, you can eat it as soon as it is done churning. It will have a soft-serve consistency as this stage; after a couple of hours in the freezer, it will set up completely.

DOES THE FROZEN YOGURT NEED TO SOFTEN BEFORE SCOOPING?

Like many premium ice creams, frozen yogurt will need a few minutes to soften before scooping if you want to get a big, perfect scoop. Freezer temperatures vary, but you can expect to be able to scoop it after a few minutes at room temperature. If you are storing your frozen yogurt in a very deep container, it may need a few extra minutes. Running your ice cream scoop under hot water before scooping will help it slide through your frozen yogurt more easily.

① CLASSIC BASES

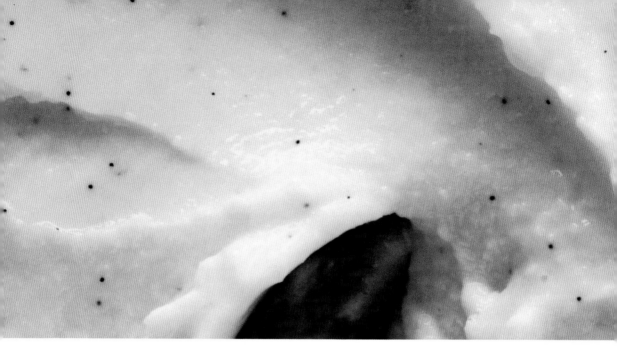

When you walk into a frozen yogurt shop, you'll probably see a wide variety of flavors that change periodically. You'll also notice that there are a handful of flavors that never change. These classic flavors appeal to just about everyone and can also serve as a platform for almost any flavor combination you can dream up. Mix-ins are a yogurt shop staple, and you shouldn't hesitate to use them with your homemade frozen yogurt as well.

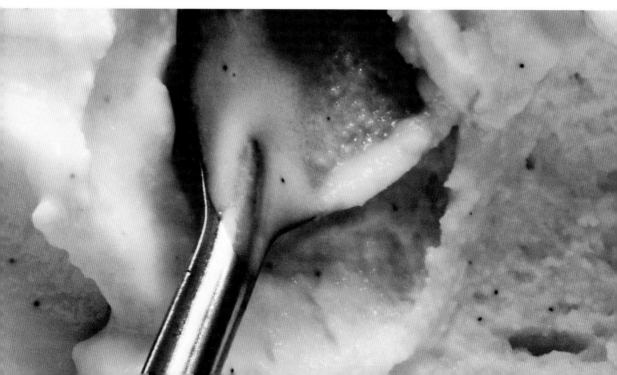

This tart, tangy frozen yogurt delivers all the flavor of plain yogurt in a slightly sweeter — and colder — package. This is a staple of every yogurt shop out there, and it is the most basic frozen yogurt you can make at home.

¼ cup water

⅔ cup sugar

2 large egg whites, room temperature

2 cups plain Greek-style yogurt, cold

1 teaspoon vanilla extract (optional)

FLAVOR TWIST

Berry Tart: Stir in chopped fresh strawberries, crushed fresh raspberries, or whole fresh blueberries (or all three!) after churning for an easy berry variation. Since you are adding the fruit after the frozen yogurt has churned, you can add as much, or as little, as you want.

1 Combine the water and sugar in a small saucepan and bring to a boil, without stirring, over medium-high heat. When the sugar mixture comes to a full boil, continue to boil for 1 minute.

2 While the sugar boils, beat the egg whites to soft peaks in a large clean bowl. When the sugar is ready, continue beating the eggs on low speed and very slowly stream in the hot sugar mixture. When all the sugar has been incorporated, turn the mixer to high and beat until the meringue is glossy and has cooled almost down to room temperature, 2 to 3 minutes. (See The Meringue Method, page 10.)

3 Put the yogurt and vanilla, if using, in a large bowl and whisk until smooth. Fold in the meringue.

4 Pour the yogurt mixture into an ice cream maker and freeze according to the manufacturer's directions.

5 Transfer to a freezer-safe container and chill in the freezer for 2 to 3 hours to allow the yogurt to completely set.

Makes about 1½ quarts

Vanilla beans have a wonderfully floral flavor and aroma that you don't find anywhere else, even with vanilla extract. Using real vanilla beans to flavor this frozen yogurt makes the vanilla the star.

1 Combine the water and sugar in a small saucepan. Split the vanilla bean lengthwise and scrape the seeds out using the back of a knife. Stir the seeds into the sugar mixture. Bring to a boil, without stirring, over medium-high heat. When the sugar mixture comes to a full boil, continue to boil for 1 minute.

2 While the sugar boils, beat the egg whites to soft peaks in a large clean bowl. When the sugar is ready, continue beating the eggs on low speed and very slowly stream in the hot sugar mixture. When all the sugar has been incorporated, turn the mixer to high and beat until the meringue is glossy and has cooled almost down to room temperature, 2 to 3 minutes. (See The Meringue Method, page 10.)

3 Whisk the yogurt in a large bowl until smooth. Fold in the meringue.

4 Pour the yogurt mixture into an ice cream maker and freeze according to the manufacturer's directions.

5 Transfer to a freezer-safe container and chill in the freezer for 2 to 3 hours to allow the yogurt to completely set.

Makes about 1½ quarts

¼ cup water

⅔ cup sugar

1 vanilla bean

2 large egg whites, room temperature

2 cups plain Greek-style yogurt, cold

FLAVOR TWISTS

Funfetti: Call to mind a popular rainbow cake by stirring in 2 tablespoons of rainbow sprinkles just after churning.

Toffee Bar Crunch: Stir in 1 cup of finely chopped chocolate-covered toffee bar candies after churning. Crush up some extra candy to sprinkle on top before serving.

TREATS TO TRY

Chocolate frozen yogurt, like tart and vanilla, is a shop staple. This version has a mild chocolate flavor that will satisfy chocolate cravings without being too rich. You'll still be able to taste some of the tanginess of the yogurt behind the cocoa, too.

1 Bring the milk to a simmer in a small saucepan. Add the cocoa powder and stir to dissolve. Set aside to cool slightly.

2 Combine the water and sugar in a small saucepan and bring to a boil, without stirring, over medium-high heat. When the sugar mixture comes to a full boil, continue to boil for 1 minute.

3 While the sugar boils, beat the egg whites to soft peaks in a large clean bowl. When the sugar is ready, continue beating the eggs on low speed and very slowly stream in the hot sugar mixture. When all the sugar has been incorporated, turn the mixer to high and beat until the meringue is glossy and has cooled almost down to room temperature, 2 to 3 minutes. (See The Meringue Method, page 10.)

4 Whisk together the yogurt, vanilla, and cocoa mixture in a large bowl until smooth. Fold in the meringue.

5 Pour the yogurt mixture into an ice cream maker and freeze according to the manufacturer's directions.

6 Transfer to a freezer-safe container and chill in the freezer for 2 to 3 hours to allow the yogurt to completely set.

Makes about 1½ quarts

½ cup whole milk

¼ cup unsweetened cocoa powder

¼ cup water

⅔ cup sugar

2 large egg whites, room temperature

2 cups plain Greek-style yogurt, cold

1 teaspoon vanilla extract

FLAVOR TWISTS

Peanut Butter Pretzel: Stir in ½ cup each of crushed pretzels and chopped peanut butter cups after churning to add a savory-sweet element, as well as a little crunch.

Chocolate Coconut Chip: Stir in 1 cup of toasted shredded coconut and ½ cup of mini chocolate chips after churning.

DARK CHOCOLATE

The rich but not-too-sweet dark chocolate flavor of this frozen yogurt will be first choice for chocoholics looking for an indulgent treat. The chocolate is melted and incorporated into the warm meringue before being folded into the yogurt. Choose a high-quality chocolate for best results.

¼ cup water

⅔ cup sugar

2 large egg whites, room temperature

4 ounces dark chocolate (60%–70% cacao), coarsely chopped

2 cups plain Greek-style yogurt, cold

2 teaspoons vanilla extract

FLAVOR TWISTS

Pick-Me-Up: Stir in 1 cup of finely crushed chocolate-covered espresso beans after churning.

Chocolate-Covered Orange: Before churning, stir in 1 tablespoon of orange liqueur. After churning, stir in ½ cup of finely chopped candied orange zest for even more citrus flavor.

1 Combine the water and sugar in a small saucepan and bring to a boil, without stirring, over medium-high heat. When the sugar mixture comes to a full boil, continue to boil for 1 minute.

2 While the sugar boils, beat the egg whites to soft peaks in a large clean bowl. When the sugar is ready, continue beating the eggs on low speed and very slowly stream in the hot sugar mixture. When all the sugar has been incorporated, turn the mixer to high and beat until the meringue is glossy and has cooled almost down to room temperature, 2 to 3 minutes. (See The Meringue Method, page 10.)

3 In a small microwave-safe bowl, melt the chocolate in the microwave, heating it in 30- to 45-second increments and stirring frequently until the chocolate is smooth. With the mixer on low speed, blend the melted chocolate into the meringue.

4 Whisk together the yogurt and vanilla in a large bowl until smooth. Fold in the meringue.

5 Pour the yogurt mixture into an ice cream maker and freeze according to the manufacturer's directions.

6 Transfer to a freezer-safe container and chill in the freezer for 2 to 3 hours to allow the yogurt to completely set.

Makes about 1½ quarts

TREATS TO TRY

CHOCOHOLIC COOKIE SANDWICHES **PAGE 99**

MUDSLIDE PIE **PAGE 120**

BLACK & WHITE CHOCOLATE POPS **PAGE 148**

Coffee delivers just as much of a pick-me-up in frozen yogurt as it does in a latte. A regular cup of coffee won't give frozen yogurt enough flavor, however, so this recipe uses instant coffee or espresso powder to give it a strong coffee punch.

1 Bring the milk to a simmer in a small saucepan. Add the coffee powder and stir to dissolve. Set aside to cool slightly.

2 Combine the water and sugar in a small saucepan and bring to a boil, without stirring, over medium-high heat. When the sugar mixture comes to a full boil, continue to boil for 1 minute.

3 While the sugar boils, beat the egg whites to soft peaks in a large clean bowl. When the sugar is ready, continue beating the eggs on low speed and very slowly stream in the hot sugar mixture. When all the sugar has been incorporated, turn the mixer to high and beat until the meringue is glossy and has cooled almost down to room temperature, 2 to 3 minutes. (See The Meringue Method, page 10.)

4 Whisk together the yogurt, vanilla, and coffee mixture in a large bowl until smooth. Fold in the meringue.

5 Pour the yogurt mixture into an ice cream maker and freeze according to the manufacturer's directions.

6 Transfer to a freezer-safe container and chill in the freezer for 2 to 3 hours to allow the yogurt to completely set.

Makes about 1½ quarts

½ cup whole milk

2 tablespoons instant coffee or espresso powder

¼ cup water

⅔ cup sugar

2 large egg whites, room temperature

2 cups plain Greek-style yogurt, cold

1 teaspoon vanilla extract

FLAVOR TWISTS
Mocha Cookies 'n' Cream: Stir in 1½ cups of crushed chocolate sandwich cookies after churning.
Caramel Macchiato: After churning, pour ½ cup of Classic Caramel Sauce (page 164) into the frozen yogurt and use a spatula to gently swirl it in, making sure that streaks of caramel sauce remain visible.

TREATS TO TRY
COFFEE LOVERS' CAKE
PAGE 108

MUDSLIDE PIE **PAGE 120**

CHOCOLATE-DIPPED COFFEE CREAM PUFFS **PAGE 158**

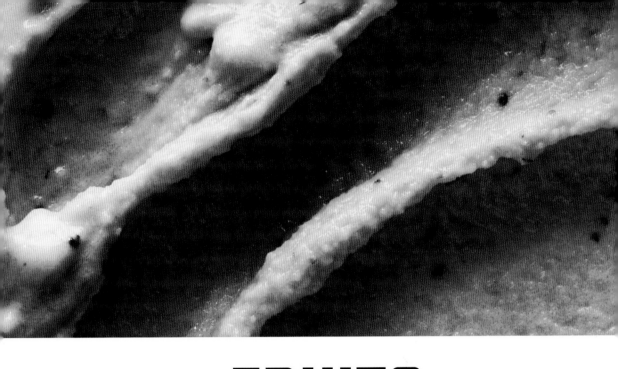

FRUITS

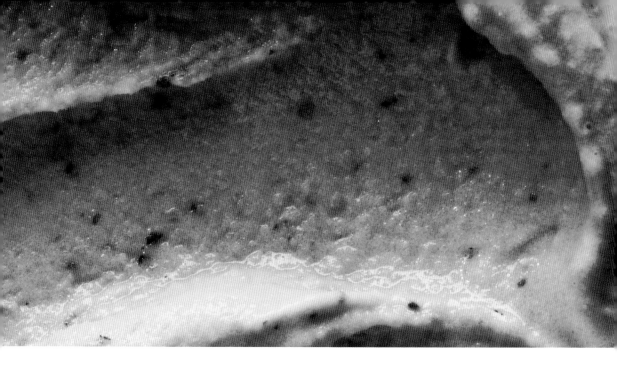

Did you know that some of the best-selling frozen yogurts are fruit-flavored? It might be because fresh fruit and plain yogurt are such a familiar — and delicious — combination that it only seems natural to combine them again for dessert. These recipes pair fruit and yogurt in a much more indulgent way than you might have thought possible.

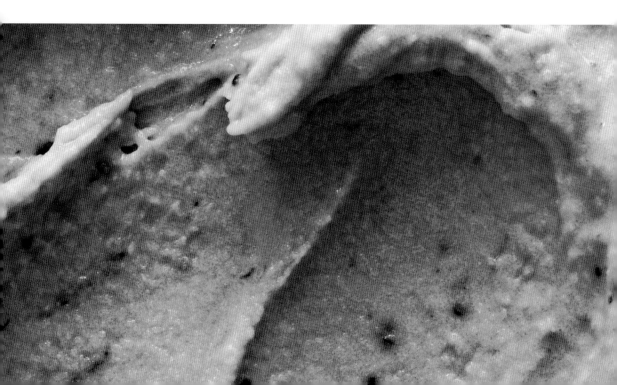

DOUBLE BLUEBERRY

Blueberries are a popular topping over plain yogurt at breakfast time, especially during the summer when blueberries are at their peak. In this frozen yogurt, the berry is showcased both as a rich sauce and in its whole form. If you don't have time to make the sauce, you can use a high-quality blueberry jam in this recipe instead.

¼ cup water

⅔ cup sugar

2 large egg whites, room temperature

2 cups plain Greek-style yogurt, cold

⅔ cup Easy Blueberry Sauce (facing page) or blueberry jam

2 teaspoons vanilla extract

¾ cup fresh blueberries

1 Combine the water and sugar in a small saucepan and bring to a boil, without stirring, over medium-high heat. When the sugar mixture comes to a full boil, continue to boil for 1 minute.

2 While the sugar boils, beat the egg whites to soft peaks in a large clean bowl. When the sugar is ready, continue beating the eggs on low speed and very slowly stream in the hot sugar mixture. When all the sugar has been incorporated, turn the mixer to high and beat until the meringue is glossy and has cooled almost down to room temperature, 2 to 3 minutes. (See The Meringue Method, page 10.)

3 Whisk together the yogurt, blueberry sauce, and vanilla in a large bowl until smooth. Fold in the meringue.

4 Pour the yogurt mixture into an ice cream maker and freeze according to the manufacturer's directions.

5 When the yogurt has finished churning and is still soft, transfer to a large bowl. Fold in the fresh blueberries until evenly distributed.

6 Transfer to a freezer-safe container and chill in the freezer for 2 to 3 hours to allow the yogurt to completely set.

Makes about 1½ quarts

EASY BLUEBERRY SAUCE

You can double this recipe and use the extra sauce as a topping with this frozen yogurt or other flavors.

Combine the blueberries, water, lemon juice, and sugar in a small saucepan and bring to a boil over medium-high heat. Cook, stirring, until the sugar has dissolved and the fruit begins to break down. Reduce the heat to medium and continue cooking until the sauce has reduced slightly, 3 to 5 minutes. Remove from the heat and cool completely before using. The sauce can be stored in an airtight container in the refrigerator for 3 to 5 days.

2 cups fresh or frozen blueberries

½ cup water

2 tablespoons fresh lemon juice

⅔ cup sugar

Makes about ⅔ cup

TREATS TO TRY

BLUEBERRY SUGAR COOKIE SANDWICHES **PAGE 97**

RED, WHITE & BLUE BOMBE **PAGE 135**

KEY LIME

Key lime pie is a dessert that translates very well to frozen yogurt because it already has a smooth, creamy filling. Adding sweetened condensed milk tempers the tanginess of the lime juice and will give your frozen yogurt that familiar flavor of the classic pie. If you can't find Key limes, you can substitute regular limes for both the lime juice and the lime zest. You will get the best flavor using fresh lime juice rather than juice from concentrate.

¼ cup water

½ cup sugar

2 large egg whites, room temperature

2 cups plain Greek-style yogurt, cold

½ cup sweetened condensed milk

⅓ cup fresh Key lime juice (4–5 Key limes)

1 teaspoon grated Key lime zest

1 Combine the water and sugar in a small saucepan and bring to a boil, without stirring, over medium-high heat. When the sugar mixture comes to a full boil, continue to boil for 1 minute.

2 While the sugar boils, beat the egg whites to soft peaks in a large clean bowl. When the sugar is ready, continue beating the eggs on low speed and very slowly stream in the hot sugar mixture. When all the sugar has been incorporated, turn the mixer to high and beat until the meringue is glossy and has cooled almost down to room temperature, 2 to 3 minutes. (See The Meringue Method, page 10.)

3 Whisk together the yogurt, condensed milk, lime juice, and lime zest in a large bowl until smooth. Fold in the meringue.

4 Pour the yogurt mixture into an ice cream maker and freeze according to the manufacturer's directions.

5 Transfer to a freezer-safe container and chill in the freezer for 2 to 3 hours to allow the yogurt to completely set.

Makes about 1½ quarts

TREAT TO TRY
KEY LIME PIE POPS
PAGE 146

The special appeal of a Creamsicle is the creamy vanilla filling surrounded by the zesty coating of orange. To get those flavors and textures in frozen yogurt, this version is flavored with a whole vanilla bean, orange zest, and orange oil — an intensely flavored extract of the same oil found in orange zest. The result is smooth, creamy, and clearly inspired by the frozen treat on a stick.

1 Combine the water and sugar in a small saucepan. Split the vanilla bean lengthwise and scrape the seeds out using the back of a knife. Add the seeds to the sugar mixture. Bring to a boil, without stirring, over medium-high heat. When the sugar mixture comes to a full boil, continue to boil for 1 minute.

2 While the sugar boils, beat the egg whites to soft peaks in a large clean bowl. When the sugar is ready, continue beating the eggs on low speed and very slowly stream in the hot sugar mixture. When all the sugar has been incorporated, turn the mixer to high and beat until the meringue is glossy and has cooled almost down to room temperature, 2 to 3 minutes. (See The Meringue Method, page 10.)

3 Whisk together the yogurt, orange zest, and orange oil in a large bowl until smooth. Fold in the meringue.

4 Pour the yogurt mixture into an ice cream maker and freeze according to the manufacturer's directions.

5 Transfer to a freezer-safe container and chill in the freezer for 2 to 3 hours to allow the yogurt to completely set.

Makes about 1½ quarts

- ¼ cup water
- ⅔ cup sugar
- 1 vanilla bean
- 2 large egg whites, room temperature
- 2 cups plain Greek-style yogurt, cold
- 1½ tablespoons grated orange zest
- ½ teaspoon orange oil

TREAT TO TRY
CREAMSICLE CUPCAKES
PAGE 116

LEMON MERINGUE

Homemade lemon curd gives this frozen yogurt the same bright lemon flavor that you look forward to in a lemon meringue pie. The difference here is that the meringue and the lemon curd are blended to create a zesty frozen treat! The lemon curd needs to be made in advance, but you can double the recipe and store the extra lemon curd to enjoy later with toast or scones for breakfast.

⅓ cup fresh lemon juice

⅔ cup sugar

2 large egg whites, room temperature

2 cups plain Greek-style yogurt, cold

⅔ cup lemon curd, homemade (facing page) or store-bought

1 Combine the lemon juice and sugar in a small saucepan and bring to a boil, without stirring, over medium-high heat. When the sugar mixture comes to a full boil, continue to boil for 1 minute.

2 While the sugar boils, beat the egg whites to soft peaks in a large clean bowl. When the sugar is ready, continue beating the eggs on low speed and very slowly stream in the hot sugar mixture. When all the sugar has been incorporated, turn the mixer to high and beat until the meringue is glossy and has cooled almost down to room temperature, 2 to 3 minutes. (See The Meringue Method, page 10.)

3 Whisk together the yogurt and lemon curd in a large bowl until smooth. Fold in the meringue.

4 Pour the yogurt mixture into an ice cream maker and freeze according to the manufacturer's directions.

5 Transfer to a freezer-safe container and chill in the freezer for 2 to 3 hours to allow the yogurt to completely set.

Makes about 1½ quarts

HOMEMADE LEMON CURD

1 Combine the lemon juice and sugar in a small saucepan and bring to a simmer over medium heat. Simmer until the sugar has completely dissolved.

2 Lightly beat the egg in a medium bowl. Whisking constantly, very slowly stream in the hot lemon syrup.

3 When all the syrup has been incorporated, pour the mixture back into the pan and cook over medium-low heat, stirring constantly, until the curd just starts to thicken and bubble at the edges. Remove from the heat and stir in the butter one piece at a time until all the butter has melted into the curd.

4 Transfer the curd to a small bowl and cover with plastic wrap, pressing it down onto the surface of the curd. Cool completely before using. The lemon curd will thicken as it cools. Leftover curd can be stored in the refrigerator for up to 1 month.

Makes about ⅔ cup

⅓ cup strained fresh lemon juice

⅓ cup sugar

1 large egg, room temperature

2 tablespoons butter, cold, cut into four pieces

MANGO

Creamy, luscious mangoes are often combined with yogurt in fruit smoothies, but they make an even better frozen yogurt. The small amount of lemon juice in this recipe brings out the natural sweetness of the mangoes.

1–2 ripe mangoes

¼ cup fresh lemon juice

⅔ cup sugar

2 large egg whites, room temperature

2 cups plain Greek-style yogurt, cold

1 Peel, pit, and coarsely chop the mangoes, and then purée in a food processor until very smooth. You should have about 1 cup of mango purée.

2 Combine the lemon juice and sugar in a small saucepan and bring to a boil, without stirring, over medium-high heat. When the sugar mixture comes to a full boil, continue to boil for 1 minute.

3 While the sugar boils, beat the egg whites to soft peaks in a large clean bowl. When the sugar is ready, continue beating the eggs on low speed and very slowly stream in the hot sugar mixture. When all the sugar has been incorporated, turn the mixer to high and beat until the meringue is glossy and has cooled almost down to room temperature, 2 to 3 minutes. (See The Meringue Method, page 10.)

4 Whisk together the yogurt and mango purée in a large bowl until smooth. Fold in the meringue.

5 Pour the yogurt mixture into an ice cream maker and freeze according to the manufacturer's directions.

6 Transfer to a freezer-safe container and chill in the freezer for 2 to 3 hours to allow the yogurt to completely set.

Makes about 1½ quarts

Strawberry is a perennial favorite at any ice cream shop, but nothing beats strawberry frozen yogurt made at home with fresh berries. The fresh strawberries shine through in this frozen yogurt and add a bright pink color.

1 Hull the strawberries, and then purée in a food processor until very smooth. You should have about 1 cup of strawberry purée.

2 Combine the water and sugar in a small saucepan and bring to a boil, without stirring, over medium-high heat. When the sugar mixture comes to a full boil, continue to boil for 1 minute.

3 While the sugar boils, beat the egg whites to soft peaks in a large clean bowl. When the sugar is ready, continue beating the eggs on low speed and very slowly stream in the hot sugar mixture. When all the sugar has been incorporated, turn the mixer to high and beat until the meringue is glossy and has cooled almost down to room temperature, 2 to 3 minutes. (See The Meringue Method, page 10.)

4 Whisk together the yogurt, strawberry purée, and vanilla in a large bowl until smooth. Fold in the meringue.

5 Pour the yogurt mixture into an ice cream maker and freeze according to the manufacturer's directions.

6 Transfer to a freezer-safe container and chill in the freezer for 2 to 3 hours to allow the yogurt to completely set.

Makes about 1½ quarts

10-12 ounces fresh strawberries

¼ cup water

⅔ cup sugar

2 large egg whites, room temperature

2 cups plain Greek-style yogurt, cold

½ teaspoon vanilla extract

FLAVOR TWIST
Strawberry Lemonade:
Before churning, add 2 teaspoons of grated lemon zest and ⅓ cup of lemon curd (home-made, page 35, or store-bought) to the frozen yogurt base.

TREATS TO TRY

STRAWBERRY CHEESECAKE

The distinctive tang of cream cheese teams up with the tartness of the yogurt to deliver a taste a lot like real cheesecake! The swirl of graham cracker crumbs brings in the final flavor element and texture of cheesecake. Fresh strawberries add great flavor to this frozen yogurt. You may substitute frozen strawberries, but be sure to thaw them completely and drain before puréeing.

10–12	ounces fresh strawberries
¼	cup water
⅔	cup sugar
2	large egg whites, room temperature
1½	cups plain Greek-style yogurt, cold
1	(8-ounce) package cream cheese, softened
1	teaspoon vanilla extract
⅔	cup graham cracker crumbs

1 Hull the strawberries, and then purée in a food processor until very smooth. You should have about 1 cup of strawberry purée.

2 Combine the water and sugar in a small saucepan and bring to a boil, without stirring, over medium-high heat. When the sugar mixture comes to a full boil, continue to boil for 1 minute.

3 While the sugar boils, beat the egg whites to soft peaks in a large clean bowl. When the sugar is ready, continue beating the eggs on low speed and very slowly stream in the hot sugar mixture. When all the sugar has been incorporated, turn the mixer to high and beat until the meringue is glossy and has cooled almost down to room temperature, 2 to 3 minutes. (See The Meringue Method, page 10.)

4 Beat together the yogurt, cream cheese, vanilla, and strawberry purée in a large bowl or food processor until smooth. If using a food processor, transfer the mixture to a large bowl. Fold in the meringue.

5 Pour the yogurt mixture into an ice cream maker and freeze according to the manufacturer's directions.

6 When the yogurt has finished churning and is still soft, transfer to a large bowl. Swirl in the graham cracker crumbs.

7 Transfer to a freezer-safe container and chill in the freezer for 2 to 3 hours to allow the yogurt to completely set.

Makes about 1½ quarts

TREAT TO TRY
STRAWBERRY CHEESECAKE BLONDIE SANDWICHES
PAGE 101

Sweet black cherries and vanilla create an unforgettable combination in ice cream and are just as delicious in frozen yogurt.

1 Coarsely chop the cherries, removing any pits. Combine the cherries and ½ cup of the sugar in a medium saucepan. Split the vanilla bean lengthwise and scrape the seeds out using the back of a knife. Stir the seeds into the cherry mixture. Bring the cherries to a boil over medium-high heat and cook, stirring occasionally, until the sugar has dissolved. Reduce the heat to medium and continue cooking until the cherries and syrup have thickened and reduced to 1 cup. Remove from the heat and set aside to cool.

2 Combine the water and remaining ½ cup sugar in a small saucepan and bring to a boil, without stirring, over medium-high heat. When the sugar mixture comes to a full boil, continue to boil for 1 minute.

3 While the sugar boils, beat the egg whites to soft peaks in a large clean bowl. When the sugar is ready, continue beating the eggs on low speed and very slowly stream in the hot sugar mixture. When all the sugar has been incorporated, turn the mixer to high and beat until the meringue is glossy and has cooled almost down to room temperature, 2 to 3 minutes. (See The Meringue Method, page 10.)

4 Whisk together the yogurt and vanilla in a large bowl until smooth. Fold in the meringue.

5 Pour the yogurt mixture into an ice cream maker and freeze according to the manufacturer's directions.

6 When the yogurt has finished churning and is still soft, transfer to a large bowl. Fold in the cherry syrup until completely incorporated.

7 Transfer to a freezer-safe container and chill in the freezer for 2 to 3 hours to allow the yogurt to completely set.

Makes about 1½ quarts

TREAT TO TRY
SPUMONI TERRINE
PAGE 131

1 cup fresh or frozen black cherries

1 cup sugar

½ vanilla bean

¼ cup water

2 large egg whites, room temperature

2 cups plain Greek-style yogurt, cold

1 teaspoon vanilla extract

FLAVOR TWIST
Chocolate Cherry Chip: To add a hint of chocolate to each bite, stir in ½ cup of finely chopped dark chocolate after churning.

BLACK CHERRY VANILLA

RICH TOASTED COCONUT

Coconut cream — the thick, almost pastelike liquid that comes from pressing fresh coconut meat and removing some of the water — gives this yogurt its richness, extra coconut flavor, and smoothness.

- 1 cup sweetened shredded coconut
- ¼ cup water
- ⅔ cup sugar
- 2 large egg whites, room temperature
- 2 cups plain Greek-style yogurt, cold
- ⅔ cup coconut cream
- 1 teaspoon vanilla extract

FLAVOR TWIST

Coco-Raspberry: After churning, stir in 1 cup of fresh raspberries and ½ cup of Raspberry Coulis (homemade, page 45, or store-bought) to add a pink, fruity swirl.

1 To toast the coconut in the oven, preheat the oven to 300°F/150°C. Spread the shredded coconut in a thin layer on a baking sheet. Bake for about 20 minutes, until the coconut is mostly golden brown, stirring every 5 minutes to make sure that the coconut browns evenly. To toast the coconut on the stove-top, spread the shredded coconut in a medium skillet and cook over medium heat, stirring frequently, for 5 to 8 minutes, until the coconut is mostly golden brown. Cool completely, then chop very finely.

2 Combine the water and sugar in a small saucepan and bring to a boil, without stirring, over medium-high heat. When the sugar mixture comes to a full boil, continue to boil for 1 minute.

3 While the sugar boils, beat the egg whites to soft peaks in a large clean bowl. When the sugar is ready, continue beating the eggs on low speed and very slowly stream in the hot sugar mixture. When all the sugar has been incorporated, turn the mixer to high and beat until the meringue is glossy and has cooled almost down to room temperature, 2 to 3 minutes. (See The Meringue Method, page 10.)

4 Whisk together the yogurt, coconut cream, and vanilla in a large bowl until very smooth. Fold in the meringue and stir in the toasted coconut.

5 Pour the yogurt mixture into an ice cream maker and freeze according to the manufacturer's directions.

6 Transfer to a freezer-safe container and chill in the freezer for 2 to 3 hours to allow the yogurt to completely set.

Makes about 1½ quarts

TREATS TO TRY

COCONUT SNOWBALL CUPCAKES
PAGE 115

PIÑA COLADA BOMBE
PAGE 136

Ice-cold watermelon is as refreshing as it gets on a hot summer day. To allow the subtle flavor of the melon to stand up to the yogurt, this recipe uses lots of fresh watermelon. Watermelon has a high water content and could give the yogurt a somewhat coarse texture if used whole, so it's best to purée it and strain out the pulp for a smooth, creamy frozen yogurt that still has a refreshing melon flavor.

1 Purée the watermelon with the lime juice in a food processor or blender. Press through a medium-fine sieve into a small bowl and set aside. Discard the solids. You should have about 1½ cups of juice. If you do not have enough juice, repeat this step with more watermelon. If you have extra juice, the excess can be added to a cocktail or smoothie.

2 Combine the water and sugar in a small saucepan and bring to a boil, without stirring, over medium-high heat. When the sugar mixture comes to a full boil, continue to boil for 1 minute.

3 While the sugar boils, beat the egg whites to soft peaks in a large clean bowl. When the sugar is ready, continue beating the eggs on low speed and very slowly stream in the hot sugar mixture. When all the sugar has been incorporated, turn the mixer to high and beat until the meringue is glossy and has cooled almost down to room temperature, 2 to 3 minutes. (See The Meringue Method, page 10.)

4 Whisk together the yogurt, watermelon juice, and liqueur, if using, in a large bowl until smooth. Fold in the meringue.

5 Pour the yogurt mixture into an ice cream maker and freeze according to the manufacturer's directions.

6 Transfer to a freezer-safe container and chill in the freezer for 2 to 3 hours to allow the yogurt to completely set.

Makes about 1½ quarts

2 cups diced watermelon

¼ cup fresh lime juice

¼ cup water

⅔ cup sugar

2 large egg whites, room temperature

2 cups plain Greek-style yogurt, cold

1 tablespoon melon liqueur (optional)

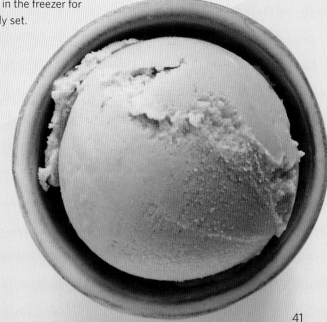

CRANBERRY

Ruby red and sweet-tart, cranberries are popular in both side dishes and desserts around the holidays. This recipe adds to the flavor lineup not only the tang of the yogurt but also a dash of almond.

CRANBERRY SAUCE

- 8 ounces fresh or frozen cranberries
- ⅓ cup water
- ¾ cup firmly packed brown sugar
- ¼ teaspoon ground allspice

- ¼ cup water
- ½ cup granulated sugar
- 2 large egg whites, room temperature
- 2 cups plain Greek-style yogurt, cold
- 1 teaspoon vanilla extract
- ¼ teaspoon almond extract

1 To make the cranberry sauce, combine the cranberries and ⅓ cup water in a medium saucepan. Cook over medium-high heat until the cranberries begin to pop, 3 to 4 minutes.

2 Add the brown sugar and allspice and continue cooking, stirring occasionally, until the sugar has dissolved and the mixture comes to a full boil. Boil, stirring occasionally, until the mixture thickens slightly, 3 to 4 minutes. Remove from the heat and set aside to cool to room temperature. The sauce can be stored in an airtight container in the refrigerator for up to 1 week.

3 Combine the remaining ¼ cup water and the granulated sugar in a small saucepan and bring to a boil, without stirring, over medium-high heat. When the sugar mixture comes to a full boil, continue to boil for 1 minute.

4 While the sugar boils, beat the egg whites to soft peaks in a large clean bowl. When the sugar is ready, continue beating the eggs on low speed and very slowly stream in the hot sugar mixture. When all the sugar has been incorporated, turn the mixer to high and beat until the meringue is glossy and has cooled almost down to room temperature, 2 to 3 minutes. (See The Meringue Method, page 10.)

5 Whisk together the yogurt, cranberry sauce, vanilla, and almond extract in a large bowl until smooth. Fold in the meringue.

6 Pour the yogurt mixture into an ice cream maker and freeze according to the manufacturer's directions.

7 Transfer to a freezer-safe container and chill in the freezer for 2 to 3 hours to allow the yogurt to completely set.

Makes about 1½ quarts

A scoop of ice cream is the perfect accompaniment to a slice of apple pie, and those same flavors are a sure hit in frozen yogurt — especially when the apple pie filling is added directly to the yogurt! Homemade apple pie filling is easy to make and delivers all the flavor of apple pie right into your yogurt. You can add some of the syrup to your yogurt base, but hold off on the apple pieces until after the churning because they will be too large for most ice cream makers to handle. The filling also makes a wonderful topping for this frozen yogurt; double its recipe to give you the extra.

1 To make the apple pie filling, combine the apples, ¼ cup granulated sugar, brown sugar, butter, cornstarch, cinnamon, ginger, allspice, and vanilla in a medium saucepan. Bring the apple mixture to a boil over medium-high heat and cook, stirring occasionally, until the sugar has dissolved. Reduce the heat to medium and continue cooking until the apples are tender and the syrup has thickened, 10 to 15 minutes. Remove from the heat and cool completely before using.

2 Combine the water and ½ cup granulated sugar in a small saucepan and bring to a boil, without stirring, over medium-high heat. When the sugar mixture comes to a full boil, continue to boil for 1 minute.

3 While the sugar boils, beat the egg whites to soft peaks in a large clean bowl. When the sugar is ready, continue beating the eggs on low speed and very slowly stream in the hot sugar mixture. When all the sugar has been incorporated, turn the mixer to high and beat until the meringue is glossy and has cooled almost down to room temperature, 2 to 3 minutes. (See The Meringue Method, page 10.)

4 Whisk together the yogurt and vanilla in a large bowl until smooth. Fold in the meringue.

5 Pour the yogurt mixture into an ice cream maker and freeze according to the manufacturer's directions.

6 When the yogurt has finished churning and is still soft, transfer to a large bowl. Fold in the filling until completely incorporated.

7 Transfer to a freezer-safe container and chill in the freezer for 2 to 3 hours to allow the yogurt to completely set.

Makes about 1½ quarts

APPLE PIE FILLING

- 1½ cups diced peeled apples
- ¼ cup granulated sugar
- ½ cup firmly packed brown sugar
- 1 tablespoon butter
- 1 tablespoon cornstarch
- 1 teaspoon ground cinnamon
- ½ teaspoon ground ginger
- ½ teaspoon ground allspice
- ½ teaspoon vanilla extract

- ¼ cup water
- ½ cup granulated sugar
- 2 large egg whites, room temperature
- 2 cups plain Greek-style yogurt, cold
- 1 teaspoon vanilla extract

TREAT TO TRY

APPLE COBBLER POPS **PAGE 144**

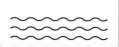

PEACH MELBA

Peach Melba is a classic dessert that combines peaches and raspberries with ice cream. It was invented at the end of the nineteenth century, and though the dessert may not seem quite as exotic as it did when ice cream and frozen desserts were still a novelty, this flavor combination never goes out of style.

3 large peaches (about 1 pound)

¼ cup water

⅔ cup sugar

2 large egg whites, room temperature

2 cups plain Greek-style yogurt, cold

2 teaspoons vanilla extract

½ cup raspberry coulis, homemade (facing page) or store-bought, plus more for serving

1 Peel and pit the peaches, and then purée in a food processor until very smooth. You should have about 1 cup of peach purée.

2 Combine the water and sugar in a small saucepan and bring to a boil, without stirring, over medium-high heat. When the sugar mixture comes to a full boil, continue to boil for 1 minute.

3 While the sugar boils, beat the egg whites to soft peaks in a large clean bowl. When the sugar is ready, continue beating the eggs on low speed and very slowly stream in the hot sugar mixture. When all the sugar has been incorporated, turn the mixer to high and beat until the meringue is glossy and has cooled almost down to room temperature, 2 to 3 minutes. (See The Meringue Method, page 10.)

4 Whisk together the yogurt, peach purée, and vanilla in a large bowl until smooth. Fold in the meringue.

5 Pour the yogurt mixture into an ice cream maker and freeze according to the manufacturer's directions.

6 When the yogurt has finished churning and is still soft, transfer to a large bowl. Swirl in the raspberry coulis.

7 Transfer to a freezer-safe container and chill in the freezer for 2 to 3 hours to allow the yogurt to completely set.

8 Drizzle each serving with 1 to 2 tablespoons of the raspberry coulis.

Makes about 1½ quarts

RASPBERRY COULIS

1 Combine the sugar, berries, and water in a medium saucepan and bring to a boil over medium-high heat. Reduce the heat to medium and cook until the fruit begins to break down and the sauce thickens, about 5 minutes. Remove from the heat and allow to cool.

2 Pour the mixture into a fine sieve over a small bowl and press, using the back of a wooden spoon. Discard the solids. Store the coulis in an airtight container in the refrigerator for up to 1 week.

Makes about 1 cup

½ cup sugar

12 ounces fresh raspberries

¼ cup water

SPICED PUMPKIN PIE

Pumpkin pie is synonymous with the fall holidays. Often served with whipped cream or ice cream, here it's captured in a frozen dessert. The cooked pumpkin mixture incorporates easily into the frozen yogurt. And even in frozen form, this dessert doesn't mind a generous topping of whipped cream.

- 1 cup canned pumpkin purée (not pumpkin pie filling)
- ⅓ cup firmly packed brown sugar
- ¼ cup whole milk
- 1 teaspoon vanilla extract
- 1 teaspoon ground cinnamon
- ½ teaspoon ground ginger
- ¼ teaspoon ground cloves
- ¼ teaspoon freshly grated nutmeg
- ¼ cup water
- ½ cup granulated sugar
- 2 large egg whites, room temperature
- 2 cups plain Greek-style yogurt, cold

1 Whisk together the pumpkin, brown sugar, milk, vanilla, cinnamon, ginger, cloves, and nutmeg in a medium saucepan. Cook, stirring constantly, over medium heat until the sugar has dissolved. Set aside to cool to room temperature.

2 Combine the water and granulated sugar in a small saucepan and bring to a boil, without stirring, over medium-high heat. When the sugar mixture comes to a full boil, continue to boil for 1 minute.

3 While the sugar boils, beat the egg whites to soft peaks in a large clean bowl. When the sugar is ready, continue beating the eggs on low speed and very slowly stream in the hot sugar mixture. When all the sugar has been incorporated, turn the mixer to high and beat until the meringue is glossy and has cooled almost down to room temperature, 2 to 3 minutes. (See The Meringue Method, page 10.)

4 Whisk together the yogurt and pumpkin mixture in a large bowl until smooth. Fold in the meringue.

5 Pour the yogurt mixture into an ice cream maker and freeze according to the manufacturer's directions.

6 Transfer to a freezer-safe container and chill in the freezer for 2 to 3 hours to allow the yogurt to completely set.

Makes about 1½ quarts

TREAT TO TRY

PUMPKIN PIE BAKED ALASKAS **PAGE 125**

FROZEN PUMPKIN PIE TERRINE **PAGE 134**

A popular dessert in the 1950s, bananas Foster was often seen at fine-dining restaurants around the country. It is made by cooking bananas in brown sugar and butter, then flambéing the mixture with a splash of dark rum. This modern frozen yogurt version doesn't pack the same flash as a flambé pan, but it captures perfectly those same great flavors.

1 Melt together the butter and brown sugar in a small saucepan or skillet over low heat. Cook, stirring, until the brown sugar has dissolved. Add the mashed banana and cook, stirring, until the mixture begins to caramelize and thicken slightly, 3 to 4 minutes. Remove from the heat and stir in the rum. Set aside.

2 Combine the water and granulated sugar in a small saucepan and bring to a boil, without stirring, over medium-high heat. When the sugar mixture comes to a full boil, continue to boil for 1 minute.

3 While the sugar boils, beat the egg whites to soft peaks in a large clean bowl. When the sugar is ready, continue beating the eggs on low speed and very slowly stream in the hot sugar mixture. When all the sugar has been incorporated, turn the mixer to high and beat until the meringue is glossy and has cooled almost down to room temperature, 2 to 3 minutes. (See The Meringue Method, page 10.)

4 Whisk together the yogurt and banana mixture in a large bowl until smooth. Fold in the meringue.

5 Pour the yogurt mixture into an ice cream maker and freeze according to the manufacturer's directions.

6 Transfer to a freezer-safe container and chill in the freezer for 2 to 3 hours to allow the yogurt to completely set.

Makes about 1½ quarts

- 3 tablespoons butter
- ⅓ cup firmly packed brown sugar
- ¾ cup mashed banana (2 ripe bananas)
- ¼ cup dark rum
- ¼ cup water
- ½ cup granulated sugar
- 2 large egg whites, room temperature
- 2 cups plain Greek-style yogurt, cold

TREAT TO TRY

CHOCOLATE PB BANANA BOMBE PAGE 139

Roasting bananas in the oven intensifies their sweetness and breaks down any of the starch that is left in the fruit, making them even creamier. Here, the creamy sweetness is paired with a salted caramel sauce that has just enough edge to satisfy a salty-sweet craving. You can use a store-bought caramel sauce or the homemade version at right.

3 medium bananas, unpeeled

¼ cup water

⅓ cup sugar

2 large egg whites, room temperature

2 cups plain Greek-style yogurt, cold

1 teaspoon vanilla extract

⅓ plus ¼ cup salted caramel sauce, homemade (facing page) or store-bought

FLAVOR TWIST

Salted Caramel: Not a banana fan? Skip the bananas in this recipe and make it as written for a rich, salted caramel frozen yogurt. Add a sprinkle of salt before serving to highlight the salt in the caramel.

1 Preheat the oven to 375°F/190°C. Line a baking sheet with aluminum foil. Place the bananas on the baking sheet and roast until black and very tender, about 25 minutes. Set aside to cool completely.

2 Combine the water and sugar in a small saucepan and bring to a boil, without stirring, over medium-high heat. When the sugar mixture comes to a full boil, continue to boil for 1 minute.

3 While the sugar boils, beat the egg whites to soft peaks in a large clean bowl. When the sugar is ready, continue beating the eggs on low speed and very slowly stream in the hot sugar mixture. When all the sugar has been incorporated, turn the mixer to high and beat until the meringue is glossy and has cooled almost down to room temperature, 2 to 3 minutes. (See The Meringue Method, page 10.)

4 Peel the roasted bananas and mash the flesh in a large bowl until very smooth. Add the yogurt, vanilla, and ¼ cup of the caramel sauce and whisk until smooth. Fold in the meringue.

5 Pour the yogurt mixture into an ice cream maker and freeze according to the manufacturer's directions.

6 When the yogurt has finished churning and is still soft, transfer to a large bowl. Drizzle in the remaining ⅓ cup caramel sauce while folding the ice cream to create a swirl.

7 Transfer to a freezer-safe container and chill in the freezer for 2 to 3 hours to allow the yogurt to completely set.

Makes about 1½ quarts

SALTED CARAMEL SAUCE

1 Combine the sugar, corn syrup, water, and a small pinch of salt in a medium saucepan and cook over medium heat, stirring with a spatula, until the sugar has dissolved.

2 When the sugar has dissolved, bring the mixture to a boil, without stirring, over medium-high heat and cook until it turns a dark caramel color, 7 to 10 minutes.

3 Combine the cream and vanilla in a small bowl or measuring cup. When the caramel has reached the desired color, remove from the heat and quickly add the cream and vanilla. The mixture will bubble vigorously and may separate. Return to the heat and cook, stirring constantly, over medium-high heat until the mixture is smooth and creamy and the ingredients are completely blended, 2 to 3 minutes. Stir in the coarse salt, then remove the caramel from the heat, scrape into another container, and cool completely before using. The caramel may be made 1 day in advance and stored in an airtight container at room temperature.

Makes about 1 cup

½ cup sugar

⅓ cup corn syrup

¼ cup water

Salt

¾ cup heavy cream

1 teaspoon vanilla extract

1 teaspoon coarse or kosher salt

TREATS TO TRY

BANANA SPLIT LAYER CAKE **PAGE 107**

CARAMEL BANANA CREAM PIE **PAGE 124**

ROASTED PINEAPPLE

A ripe pineapple is delicious when it is fresh, but roasted pineapple is even better. Roasted pineapple has an intensely tropical flavor, thanks to the fact that the sugars in the fruit concentrate while it cooks. I add a little bit of brown sugar to the pineapple to help it along, too. The roasted pineapple can be prepared a couple of days in advance and stored in the refrigerator until you're ready to use it.

2 cups fresh or frozen pineapple chunks, thawed if frozen

¼ cup firmly packed brown sugar

¼ cup water

⅓ cup granulated sugar

2 large egg whites, room temperature

2 cups plain Greek-style yogurt, cold

1 teaspoon vanilla extract

1 Preheat the oven to 375°F/190°C. Line a baking sheet with parchment paper. Toss the pineapple chunks with the brown sugar in a medium bowl. Arrange on the baking sheet and roast for 20 to 30 minutes, until the pineapple is golden and tender. Set aside to cool completely, then purée in a food processor or blender.

2 Combine the water and granulated sugar in a small saucepan and bring to a boil, without stirring, over medium-high heat. When the sugar mixture comes to a full boil, continue to boil for 1 minute.

3 While the sugar boils, beat the egg whites to soft peaks in a large clean bowl. When the sugar is ready, continue beating the eggs on low speed and very slowly stream in the hot sugar mixture. When all the sugar has been incorporated, turn the mixer to high and beat until the meringue is glossy and has cooled almost down to room temperature, 2 to 3 minutes. (See The Meringue Method, page 10.)

4 Combine the yogurt, pineapple purée, and vanilla in a large bowl. Fold in the meringue.

5 Pour the yogurt mixture into an ice cream maker and freeze according to the manufacturer's directions.

6 Transfer to a freezer-safe container and chill in the freezer for 2 to 3 hours to allow the yogurt to completely set.

Makes about 1½ quarts

TREAT TO TRY
PIÑA COLADA BOMBE
PAGE 136

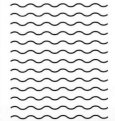

The rich creaminess of a perfectly ripe avocado is the very same quality that is so appealing in ice cream and frozen yogurt, so it's hard to lose when this tropical fruit features in a cold dessert or drink. Here the avocado is paired with honey, the perfect natural sweetener to complement the nutty character of this fruit.

1 Pit and peel the avocados, and then purée in a food processor or mash until very smooth. You should have about 1 cup of avocado purée.

2 Combine the water and sugar in a small saucepan and bring to a boil, without stirring, over medium-high heat. When the sugar mixture comes to a full boil, continue to boil for 1 minute.

3 While the sugar boils, beat the egg whites to soft peaks in a large clean bowl. When the sugar is ready, continue beating the eggs on low speed and very slowly stream in the hot sugar mixture. When all the sugar has been incorporated, turn the mixer to high and beat until the meringue is glossy and has cooled almost down to room temperature, 2 to 3 minutes. (See The Meringue Method, page 10.)

4 Whisk together the yogurt, avocado purée, honey, and vanilla in a large bowl until smooth. Fold in the meringue.

5 Pour the yogurt mixture into an ice cream maker and freeze according to the manufacturer's directions.

6 Transfer to a freezer-safe container and chill in the freezer for 2 to 3 hours to allow the yogurt to completely set.

Makes about 1½ quarts

2 large ripe avocados
¼ cup water
½ cup sugar
2 large egg whites, room temperature
2 cups plain Greek-style yogurt, cold
⅓ cup honey
1 teaspoon vanilla extract

③ SUGAR AND SPICES

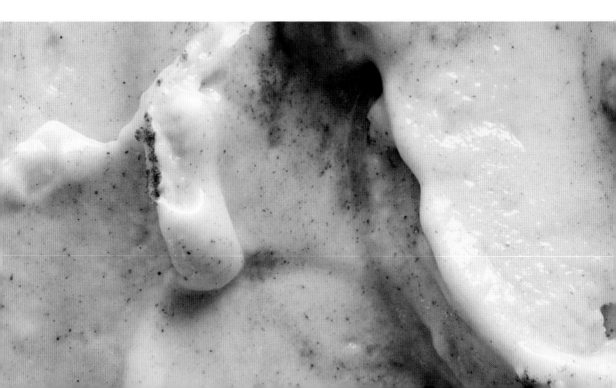

Sugar and spice make everything nice — when it comes to adding a few new layers of flavor to your frozen yogurt, that is! This chapter will have you raiding your pantry for ingredients to create unforgettable and unexpected frozen yogurt flavors.

GINGER & CARDAMOM

Spicy ginger and bright, floral cardamom come together with a hint of lemon and vanilla in this frozen yogurt. The combination of ginger and cardamom is enough to give any dish an exotic twist, and this is no exception. Be sure to strain out the fibrous ginger before churning the base.

½ cup whole milk

3 whole cardamom pods, crushed

2 tablespoons grated fresh ginger

1 teaspoon grated lemon zest

¼ cup water

⅔ cup sugar

2 large egg whites, room temperature

2 cups plain Greek-style yogurt, cold

1 teaspoon vanilla extract

1 Combine the milk, cardamom, ginger, and lemon zest in a small saucepan and bring to a simmer. Remove from the heat and allow the spices to steep for 30 minutes.

2 Strain the spice-infused milk into a clean bowl and set aside. Discard the solids.

3 Combine the water and sugar in a small saucepan and bring to a boil, without stirring, over medium-high heat. When the sugar mixture comes to a full boil, continue to boil for 1 minute.

4 While the sugar boils, beat the egg whites to soft peaks in a large clean bowl. When the sugar is ready, continue beating the eggs on low speed and very slowly stream in the hot sugar mixture. When all the sugar has been incorporated, turn the mixer to high and beat until the meringue is glossy and has cooled almost down to room temperature, 2 to 3 minutes. (See The Meringue Method, page 10.)

5 Whisk together the yogurt, vanilla, and spice-infused milk in a large bowl until smooth. Fold in the meringue.

6 Pour the yogurt mixture into an ice cream maker and freeze according to the manufacturer's directions.

7 Transfer to a freezer-safe container and chill in the freezer for 2 to 3 hours to allow the yogurt to completely set.

Makes about 1½ quarts

TREAT TO TRY
GINGER SPICE COOKIE SANDWICHES PAGE 98

Chai tea is made with a wide variety of spices and is known for its complex flavor. This frozen yogurt is infused with some of those distinctive flavors that make the tea so delicious. Ground rather than crushed spices make the process easier.

1 Bring the milk to a simmer in a small saucepan over medium heat. Combine the cinnamon, ginger, allspice, cardamom, and cloves with 1 teaspoon of the vanilla and the almond extract in a small heatproof bowl. Pour the hot milk over the spice mixture and stir well. Let steep undisturbed for 1 hour. (Most of the spices will sink to the bottom.)

2 Combine the water and sugar in a small saucepan and bring to a boil, without stirring, over medium-high heat. When the sugar mixture comes to a full boil, continue to boil for 1 minute.

3 While the sugar boils, beat the egg whites to soft peaks in a large clean bowl. When the sugar is ready, continue beating the eggs on low speed and very slowly stream in the hot sugar mixture. When all the sugar has been incorporated, turn the mixer to high and beat until the meringue is glossy and has cooled almost down to room temperature, 2 to 3 minutes. (See The Meringue Method, page 10.)

4 Whisk together the yogurt, the remaining 1 teaspoon vanilla, and the spice-infused milk in a large bowl until smooth, being careful to get any of the spice mixture at the bottom of the bowl. Fold in the meringue.

5 Pour the yogurt mixture into an ice cream maker and freeze according to the manufacturer's directions.

6 Transfer to a freezer-safe container and chill in the freezer for 2 to 3 hours to allow the yogurt to completely set.

Makes about 1½ quarts

1 cup whole milk

1½ teaspoons ground cinnamon

1 teaspoon ground ginger

½ teaspoon ground allspice

½ teaspoon ground cardamom

¼ teaspoon ground cloves

2 teaspoons vanilla extract

¼ teaspoon almond extract

¼ cup water

⅔ cup sugar

2 large egg whites, room temperature

2 cups plain Greek-style yogurt, cold

EARL GREY

Earl Grey tea is comfort in a cup for many tea lovers. Its distinctive flavor comes from the peel of the bergamot orange, complemented here by the addition of a fragrant vanilla bean. You can use vanilla extract instead, but the combination of the vanilla bean and the Earl Grey tea is like a match made in heaven.

⅔ cup whole milk

6 Earl Grey tea bags

1 vanilla bean

¼ cup water

⅔ cup sugar

2 large egg whites, room temperature

2 cups plain Greek-style yogurt, cold

1 Combine the milk and tea bags in a small saucepan. Split the vanilla bean lengthwise and scrape the seeds out using the back of a knife. Add the seeds to the milk and bring the mixture to a simmer over medium heat. Turn off the heat and allow the tea bags to steep for 15 minutes. Remove the tea bags and allow the mixture to cool to room temperature.

2 Combine the water and sugar in a small saucepan and bring to a boil, without stirring, over medium-high heat. When the sugar mixture comes to a full boil, continue to boil for 1 minute.

3 While the sugar boils, beat the egg whites to soft peaks in a large clean bowl. When the sugar is ready, continue beating the eggs on low speed and very slowly stream in the hot sugar mixture. When all the sugar has been incorporated, turn the mixer to high and beat until the meringue is glossy and has cooled almost down to room temperature, 2 to 3 minutes. (See The Meringue Method, page 10.)

4 Whisk together the yogurt and tea-infused milk in a large bowl until smooth. Fold in the meringue.

5 Pour the yogurt mixture into an ice cream maker and freeze according to the manufacturer's directions.

6 Transfer to a freezer-safe container and chill in the freezer for 2 to 3 hours to allow the yogurt to completely set.

Makes about 1½ quarts

The mint julep cocktail is the traditional drink served at the running of the Kentucky Derby every year. This frozen yogurt variation combines mint, bourbon, and vanilla for a flavor that is surprisingly refreshing and very grown-up.

1 Combine the water and sugar in a small saucepan and bring to a boil, without stirring, over medium-high heat. When the sugar mixture comes to a full boil, continue to boil for 1 minute.

2 While the sugar boils, beat the egg whites to soft peaks in a large clean bowl. When the sugar is ready, continue beating the eggs on low speed and very slowly stream in the hot sugar mixture. When all the sugar has been incorporated, turn the mixer to high and beat until the meringue is glossy and has cooled almost down to room temperature, 2 to 3 minutes. (See The Meringue Method, page 10.)

3 Whisk together the yogurt, bourbon, vanilla, and peppermint extract in a large bowl until smooth. Fold in the meringue.

4 Pour the yogurt mixture into an ice cream maker and freeze according to the manufacturer's directions.

5 Transfer to a freezer-safe container and chill in the freezer for 2 to 3 hours to allow the yogurt to completely set.

Makes about 1½ quarts

¼ cup water

½ cup sugar

2 large egg whites, room temperature

2 cups plain Greek-style yogurt, cold

¼ cup bourbon

1 teaspoon vanilla extract

1 teaspoon peppermint extract

GRASSHOPPER

The grasshopper cocktail first became popular in the 1950s and '60s as an after-dinner drink. It features white crème de cacao and crème de menthe, which give it the refreshing chocolate-mint flavor and distinctive bright green color for which it's known. You'll find those same great flavors in this frozen yogurt, but you might want to give it a little food coloring to boost the cocktail's signature green hue.

¼ cup water

⅔ cup sugar

2 large egg whites, room temperature

2 cups plain Greek-style yogurt, cold

2 tablespoons white crème de cacao

2 tablespoons crème de menthe

½ teaspoon peppermint extract

½ teaspoon green food coloring (optional)

1 Combine the water and sugar in a small saucepan and bring to a boil, without stirring, over medium-high heat. When the sugar mixture comes to a full boil, continue to boil for 1 minute.

2 While the sugar boils, beat the egg whites to soft peaks in a large clean bowl. When the sugar is ready, continue beating the eggs on low speed and very slowly stream in the hot sugar mixture. When all the sugar has been incorporated, turn the mixer to high and beat until the meringue is glossy and has cooled almost down to room temperature, 2 to 3 minutes. (See The Meringue Method, page 10.)

3 Whisk together the yogurt, crème de cacao, crème de menthe, and peppermint extract in a large bowl until smooth. Whisk in the food coloring, if using. Fold in the meringue.

4 Pour the yogurt mixture into an ice cream maker and freeze according to the manufacturer's directions.

5 Transfer to a freezer-safe container and chill in the freezer for 2 to 3 hours to allow the yogurt to completely set.

Makes about 1½ quarts

Matcha is a brightly colored, finely milled green tea powder that is also popular in many culinary applications because of its bold color and distinctive, slightly bitter flavor. It can be found at Asian markets and is also available at many specialty grocers and tea shops. The tanginess of the Greek yogurt is a good match for the flavor of the matcha, and there is just enough sweetness to create the perfect balance.

1 Bring the milk to a simmer in a small saucepan. Add the matcha powder and stir to dissolve. Set aside and allow to cool to room temperature.

2 Combine the water and sugar in a small saucepan and bring to a boil, without stirring, over medium-high heat. When the sugar mixture comes to a full boil, continue to boil for 1 minute.

3 While the sugar boils, beat the egg whites to soft peaks in a large clean bowl. When the sugar is ready, continue beating the eggs on low speed and very slowly stream in the hot sugar mixture. When all the sugar has been incorporated, turn the mixer to high and beat until the meringue is glossy and has cooled almost down to room temperature, 2 to 3 minutes. (See The Meringue Method, page 10.)

4 Whisk together the yogurt, vanilla, and matcha-infused milk in a large bowl until smooth. Fold in the meringue.

5 Pour the yogurt mixture into an ice cream maker and freeze according to the manufacturer's directions.

6 Transfer to a freezer-safe container and chill in the freezer for 2 to 3 hours to allow the yogurt to completely set.

Makes about 1½ quarts

½ cup whole milk

3 tablespoons matcha powder

¼ cup water

⅔ cup sugar

2 large egg whites, room temperature

2 cups plain Greek-style yogurt, cold

1 teaspoon vanilla extract

FLAVOR TWIST
Coconut Matcha: Substitute unsweetened coconut cream for the milk in the recipe, then make the frozen yogurt as directed. After churning, stir in ¾ cup of sweetened shredded coconut to add some texture and more coconut flavor.

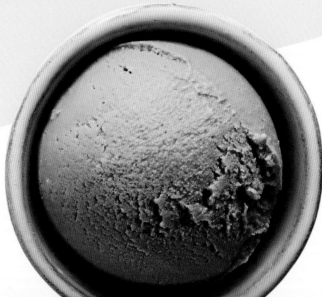

COOKIE BUTTER

Biscoff spread has the creamy consistency of peanut butter but is made from buttery cookies flavored with brown sugar and spices. It is thick, sweet, and downright addictive — especially when it's mixed into frozen yogurt, where it gives the plain yogurt a rich texture and brown sugar sweetness. The addition of crushed Biscoff cookies packs in more of that irresistible flavor and also a bit of crunch for contrast.

¼ cup water

½ cup sugar

2 large egg whites, room temperature

2 cups plain Greek-style yogurt, cold

¾ cup Biscoff spread

1 teaspoon vanilla extract

¾ cup crushed Biscoff cookies

1 Combine the water and sugar in a small saucepan and bring to a boil, without stirring, over medium-high heat. When the sugar mixture comes to a full boil, continue to boil for 1 minute.

2 While the sugar boils, beat the egg whites to soft peaks in a large clean bowl. When the sugar is ready, continue beating the eggs on low speed and very slowly stream in the hot sugar mixture. When all the sugar has been incorporated, turn the mixer to high and beat until the meringue is glossy and has cooled almost down to room temperature, 2 to 3 minutes. (See The Meringue Method, page 10.)

3 Beat together the yogurt, Biscoff spread, and vanilla in a large bowl until smooth. Fold in the meringue.

4 Pour the yogurt mixture into an ice cream maker and freeze according to the manufacturer's directions.

5 When the yogurt has finished churning and is still soft, transfer to a large bowl. Stir in the crushed Biscoff cookies until evenly distributed.

6 Transfer to a freezer-safe container and chill in the freezer for 2 to 3 hours to allow the yogurt to completely set.

Makes about 1½ quarts

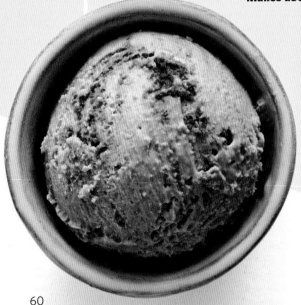

TREAT TO TRY

GINGER SPICE COOKIE SANDWICHES **PAGE 98**

The rich, nutty flavor of browned butter is even better when it is combined with vanilla, as in this original and truly decadent frozen yogurt.

1 Place the butter in a small saucepan and melt over medium heat until the butter bubbles and foams, 3 to 4 minutes. When the foam has subsided, it will begin to brown and release a nutty smell. Stir the butter with a spatula as it browns to prevent burning, scraping the brown bits off the bottom of the pan. Cook and stir until the butter is golden brown, 1 to 3 minutes. Transfer to a small bowl and set aside to cool to room temperature.

2 Combine the water and sugar in a small saucepan. Split the vanilla bean lengthwise and scrape the seeds out using the back of a knife. Add the seeds to the sugar mixture. Bring to a boil, without stirring, over medium-high heat. When the sugar mixture comes to a full boil, continue to boil for 1 minute.

3 While the sugar boils, beat the egg whites to soft peaks in a large clean bowl. When the sugar is ready, continue beating the eggs on low speed and very slowly stream in the hot sugar mixture. When all the sugar has been incorporated, turn the mixer to high and beat until the meringue is glossy and has cooled almost down to room temperature, 2 to 3 minutes. (See The Meringue Method, page 10.)

4 Whisk together the yogurt and browned butter in a large bowl until smooth. Fold in the meringue.

5 Pour the yogurt mixture into an ice cream maker and freeze according to the manufacturer's directions.

6 Transfer to a freezer-safe container and chill in the freezer for 2 to 3 hours to allow the yogurt to completely set.

Makes about 1½ quarts

5 tablespoons plus
   1 teaspoon butter

¼ cup water

⅔ cup sugar

1 vanilla bean

2 large egg whites,
   room temperature

2 cups plain Greek-
   style yogurt, cold

TREAT TO TRY
CINNAMON BUN POPS
PAGE 145

DULCE DE LECHE

Dulce de leche is a thick, milky caramel sauce that is made by caramelizing sweetened condensed milk. Its rich flavor is decadent, and it is a popular ingredient in many Latin American desserts.

¼ cup water

½ cup sugar

2 large egg whites, room temperature

2 cups plain Greek-style yogurt, cold

½ cup dulce de leche, homemade (facing page) or store-bought

1 teaspoon vanilla extract

¼ teaspoon salt

1 Combine the water and sugar in a small saucepan and bring to a boil, without stirring, over medium-high heat. When the sugar mixture comes to a full boil, continue to boil for 1 minute.

2 While the sugar boils, beat the egg whites to soft peaks in a large clean bowl. When the sugar is ready, continue beating the eggs on low speed and very slowly stream in the hot sugar mixture. When all the sugar has been incorporated, turn the mixer to high and beat until the meringue is glossy and has cooled almost down to room temperature, 2 to 3 minutes. (See The Meringue Method, page 10.)

3 Beat together the yogurt, dulce de leche, vanilla, and salt in a large bowl until smooth. Fold in the meringue.

4 Pour the yogurt mixture into an ice cream maker and freeze according to the manufacturer's directions.

5 Transfer to a freezer-safe container and chill in the freezer for 2 to 3 hours to allow the yogurt to completely set.

Makes about 1½ quarts

DULCE DE LECHE

1 Set up a double boiler by bringing a pot of water to a simmer and placing a heatproof bowl over the water, without the bowl touching the water. Pour the milk into the bowl and cook, stirring occasionally to maintain a smooth consistency, until the milk is thick and deep golden, 60 to 70 minutes. Be careful not to let all the water cook off; if the water level in the pot becomes too low, replenish with additional hot water.

2 Remove the bowl from the heat and cool completely before using. The dulce de leche can be made 1 to 2 days in advance and stored in an airtight container at room temperature.

Makes about 1 cup

1 (14-ounce) can sweetened condensed milk

TREAT TO TRY
SALTED CARAMEL SWIRL
BONBONS **PAGE 151**

MAPLE SYRUP

The rich, sweet flavor of maple syrup stands out in this frozen yogurt. Be sure to choose Grade A: Dark Color and Robust Flavor maple syrup, which is darker in color and will give you the richest maple syrup flavor. Don't be tempted to substitute inexpensive pancake syrup, a product that's made with maple-flavored corn syrup and is not the real thing.

¼ cup water

½ cup sugar

2 large egg whites, room temperature

2 cups plain Greek-style yogurt, cold

½ cup maple syrup

½ teaspoon vanilla extract

FLAVOR TWIST

Maple Nut: Stir in ¾ cup of chopped toasted walnuts or pecans after churning to add a nutty crunch. For an extra-sweet treat, you can even use candied nuts!

1 Combine the water and sugar in a small saucepan and bring to a boil, without stirring, over medium-high heat. When the sugar mixture comes to a full boil, continue to boil for 1 minute.

2 While the sugar boils, beat the egg whites to soft peaks in a large clean bowl. When the sugar is ready, continue beating the eggs on low speed and very slowly stream in the hot sugar mixture. When all the sugar has been incorporated, turn the mixer to high and beat until the meringue is glossy and has cooled almost down to room temperature, 2 to 3 minutes. (See The Meringue Method, page 10.)

3 Whisk together the yogurt, maple syrup, and vanilla in a large bowl until smooth. Fold in the meringue.

4 Pour the yogurt mixture into an ice cream maker and freeze according to the manufacturer's directions.

5 Transfer to a freezer-safe container and chill in the freezer for 2 to 3 hours to allow the yogurt to completely set.

Makes about 1½ quarts

Honey is the most popular way to top off a bowl of Greek-style yogurt, since the intense natural sweetness of the honey contrasts well with the tanginess of the yogurt. Honey is sweet, but that sweetness is what will keep you coming back for seconds.

1 Combine the water and sugar in a small saucepan and bring to a boil, without stirring, over medium-high heat. When the sugar mixture comes to a full boil, continue to boil for 1 minute.

2 While the sugar boils, beat the egg whites to soft peaks in a large clean bowl. When the sugar is ready, continue beating the eggs on low speed and very slowly stream in the hot sugar mixture. When all the sugar has been incorporated, turn the mixer to high and beat until the meringue is glossy and has cooled almost down to room temperature, 2 to 3 minutes. (See The Meringue Method, page 10.)

3 Whisk together the yogurt, honey, and vanilla in a large bowl until smooth. Fold in the meringue.

4 Pour the yogurt mixture into an ice cream maker and freeze according to the manufacturer's directions.

5 Transfer to a freezer-safe container and chill in the freezer for 2 to 3 hours to allow the yogurt to completely set.

Makes about 1½ quarts

¼ cup water

½ cup sugar

2 large egg whites, room temperature

2 cups plain Greek-style yogurt, cold

½ cup honey

2 teaspoons vanilla extract

MAPLE BACON

Maple syrup and bacon are terrific at breakfast, and the salty-sweet pair is great in frozen yogurt, too. Cut the cooked bacon into tiny pieces before adding it to the yogurt base to preserve its crispness and add a little crunch.

2 ounces bacon, uncooked (3–4 slices)

¼ cup water

½ cup sugar

2 large egg whites, room temperature

2 cups plain Greek-style yogurt, cold

½ cup maple syrup

½ teaspoon vanilla extract

1 Cook the bacon in a large skillet over medium heat until completely crisp. Drain on a plate lined with paper towels and cool completely. Chop into very small bits and set aside.

2 Combine the water and sugar in a small saucepan and bring to a boil, without stirring, over medium-high heat. When the sugar mixture comes to a full boil, continue to boil for 1 minute.

3 While the sugar boils, beat the egg whites to soft peaks in a large clean bowl. When the sugar is ready, continue beating the eggs on low speed and very slowly stream in the hot sugar mixture. When all the sugar has been incorporated, turn the mixer to high and beat until the meringue is glossy and has cooled almost down to room temperature, 2 to 3 minutes. (See The Meringue Method, page 10.)

4 Whisk together the yogurt, maple syrup, and vanilla in a large bowl until smooth. Fold in the meringue and the chopped bacon.

5 Pour the yogurt mixture into an ice cream maker and freeze according to the manufacturer's directions.

6 Transfer to a freezer-safe container and chill in the freezer for 2 to 3 hours to allow the yogurt to completely set.

Makes about 1½ quarts

Goat cheese, much like cream cheese, is a soft cheese that adds a particular flavor and texture to many desserts. This frozen yogurt brings together honey and goat cheese for a delicious pairing.

¼ cup water

½ cup sugar

2 large egg whites, room temperature

2 cups plain Greek-style yogurt, cold

⅓ cup goat cheese, softened

⅓ cup honey

2 teaspoons vanilla extract

FLAVOR TWIST

Berries 'n' Honey: Fold 1 cup of fresh blueberries into the frozen yogurt after churning to add a pop of color and bright flavor that will contrast well with the sweetness of the honey.

1 Combine the water and sugar in a small saucepan and bring to a boil, without stirring, over medium-high heat. When the sugar mixture comes to a full boil, continue to boil for 1 minute.

2 While the sugar boils, beat the egg whites to soft peaks in a large clean bowl. When the sugar is ready, continue beating the eggs on low speed and very slowly stream in the hot sugar mixture. When all the sugar has been incorporated, turn the mixer to high and beat until the meringue is glossy and has cooled almost down to room temperature, 2 to 3 minutes. (See The Meringue Method, page 10.)

3 Beat together the yogurt, cheese, honey, and vanilla in a large bowl or food processor until smooth. If using a food processor, transfer the mixture to a large bowl. Fold in the meringue.

4 Pour the yogurt mixture into an ice cream maker and freeze according to the manufacturer's directions.

5 Transfer to a freezer-safe container and chill in the freezer for 2 to 3 hours to allow the yogurt to completely set.

Makes about 1½ quarts

This frozen yogurt flavor was inspired by the classic bake sale cookie, known for its distinctive cinnamon-sugar flavor. The base is flavored with cinnamon, and a cinnamon-sugar swirl is added to the frozen yogurt just after churning. The sugar will mostly dissolve into the yogurt as it sits in the freezer, but it will leave behind an attractive swirl and a sweet cinnamon flavor that will remind you of a real snickerdoodle.

¼ cup water

⅔ plus ¼ cup sugar

2 large egg whites, room temperature

2 cups plain Greek-style yogurt, cold

2 teaspoons vanilla extract

2 teaspoons ground cinnamon

1 Combine the water and ⅔ cup of the sugar in a small saucepan and bring to a boil, without stirring, over medium-high heat. When the sugar mixture comes to a full boil, continue to boil for 1 minute.

2 While the sugar boils, beat the egg whites to soft peaks in a large clean bowl. When the sugar is ready, continue beating the eggs on low speed and very slowly stream in the hot sugar mixture. When all the sugar has been incorporated, turn the mixer to high and beat until the meringue is glossy and has cooled almost down to room temperature, 2 to 3 minutes. (See The Meringue Method, page 10.)

3 Whisk together the yogurt, vanilla, and 1 teaspoon of the cinnamon in a large bowl. Fold in the meringue.

4 Pour the yogurt mixture into an ice cream maker and freeze according to the manufacturer's directions.

5 While the frozen yogurt is churning, combine the remaining ¼ cup sugar and the remaining 1 teaspoon cinnamon in a small bowl.

6 When the yogurt has finished churning and is still soft, transfer it to a large bowl. Sprinkle in the cinnamon-sugar mixture while folding the yogurt to create a swirl.

7 Transfer to a freezer-safe container and chill in the freezer for 2 to 3 hours to allow the yogurt to completely set.

Makes about 1½ quarts

TREAT TO TRY
SNICKERDOODLE LAYER CAKE PAGE 111

TIRAMISU

This Italian classic makes for a fantastic frozen yogurt flavor in which sweet-tart yogurt takes the place of the traditional mascarpone cheese. There are two types of ladyfingers commonly available at stores: crispy and soft. You can use either style, but if you get the crispier cookies, you may need to soak them in the coffee mixture for a few extra seconds to soften them.

¼ cup water

⅔ plus ¼ cup sugar

2 large egg whites, room temperature

2 cups plain Greek-style yogurt, cold

2 teaspoons vanilla extract

½ cup strong, hot coffee

2 tablespoons dark rum (optional)

12–15 ladyfingers

1 Combine the water and ⅔ cup of the sugar in a small saucepan and bring to a boil, without stirring, over medium-high heat. When the sugar mixture comes to a full boil, continue to boil for 1 minute.

2 While the sugar boils, beat the egg whites to soft peaks in a large clean bowl. When the sugar is ready, continue beating the eggs on low speed and very slowly stream in the hot sugar mixture. When all the sugar has been incorporated, turn the mixer to high and beat until the meringue is glossy and has cooled almost down to room temperature, 2 to 3 minutes. (See The Meringue Method, page 10.)

3 Whisk together the yogurt and vanilla in a large bowl until smooth. Fold in the meringue.

4 Pour the yogurt mixture into an ice cream maker and freeze according to the manufacturer's directions.

5 Pour half of the frozen yogurt into a 9-inch square pan, spreading it into an even layer. Combine the remaining ¼ cup sugar and the hot coffee in a small bowl and stir until the sugar has dissolved. Add the rum, if using. Dip the ladyfingers into the coffee mixture until saturated, 2 or 3 seconds. Arrange the ladyfingers over the frozen yogurt, then top with the remaining frozen yogurt.

6 Freeze for at least 2 to 3 hours to allow the yogurt to completely set before serving. When scooping, be sure to scoop deep enough to get both ladyfingers and frozen yogurt in each scoop.

Makes about 1½ quarts

Candy canes are instantly recognizable, and this peppermint frozen yogurt sports the same swirled look with the help of a little food coloring. The optional splash of peppermint schnapps boosts the peppermint flavor in this dessert and makes it a little more grown-up, while bits of chopped peppermint or candy cane offer a nice crunch.

1 Combine the water and sugar in a small saucepan and bring to a boil, without stirring, over medium-high heat. When the sugar mixture comes to a full boil, continue to boil for 1 minute.

2 While the sugar boils, beat the egg whites to soft peaks in a large clean bowl. When the sugar is ready, continue beating the eggs on low speed and very slowly stream in the hot sugar mixture. When all the sugar has been incorporated, turn the mixer to high and beat until the meringue is glossy and has cooled almost down to room temperature, 2 to 3 minutes. (See The Meringue Method, page 10.)

3 Whisk together the yogurt, schnapps (if using), vanilla, and peppermint extract in a large bowl until smooth. Fold in the meringue.

4 Pour the yogurt mixture into an ice cream maker and freeze according to the manufacturer's directions.

5 When the yogurt has finished churning and is still soft, transfer to a large bowl. Set aside ½ cup in a small bowl. Fold the crushed peppermint into the yogurt in the large bowl. Stir the food coloring into the yogurt in the small bowl until well incorporated. Fold the red-tinted yogurt into the yogurt in the large bowl to create a swirled effect.

6 Transfer to a freezer-safe container and chill in the freezer for 2 to 3 hours to allow the yogurt to completely set.

Makes about 1½ quarts

¼ cup water

⅔ cup sugar

2 large egg whites, room temperature

2 cups plain Greek-style yogurt, cold

2 tablespoons peppermint schnapps (optional)

1 teaspoon vanilla extract

1 teaspoon peppermint extract

½ cup crushed peppermint candies or candy canes

¼ teaspoon red food coloring

TREAT TO TRY

CANDY CANE BROWNIE SANDWICHES **PAGE 103**

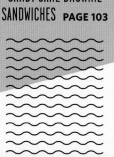

EGGNOG

Thick, rich eggnog, perfumed by nutmeg and vanilla, is a holiday staple, and this frozen version is a cool way to enjoy it. Freshly grated nutmeg and vanilla make the eggnog pop, and the splash of bourbon or dark rum supplies the same warming kick as the classic drink. If you want to skip the alcohol in this recipe, you can omit it and substitute 1 teaspoon of rum extract instead.

¼ cup water

⅔ cup sugar

2 large egg whites, room temperature

2 cups plain Greek-style yogurt, cold

1 cup eggnog

2 tablespoons bourbon or dark rum (optional)

2 teaspoons vanilla extract

½ teaspoon freshly grated nutmeg

1 Combine the water and sugar in a small saucepan and bring to a boil, without stirring, over medium-high heat. When the sugar mixture comes to a full boil, continue to boil for 1 minute.

2 While the sugar boils, beat the egg whites to soft peaks in a large clean bowl. When the sugar is ready, continue beating the eggs on low speed and very slowly stream in the hot sugar mixture. When all the sugar has been incorporated, turn the mixer to high and beat until the meringue is glossy and has cooled almost down to room temperature, 2 to 3 minutes. (See The Meringue Method, page 10.)

3 Whisk together the yogurt, eggnog, bourbon (if using), vanilla, and nutmeg in a large bowl until smooth. Fold in the meringue.

4 Pour the yogurt mixture into an ice cream maker and freeze according to the manufacturer's directions.

5 Transfer to a freezer-safe container and chill in the freezer for 2 to 3 hours to allow the yogurt to completely set.

Makes about 1½ quarts

Sweet, spicy gingerbread is another confection that evokes the holidays. Most gingerbreads include molasses, brown sugar, ginger, and cinnamon. This version calls for a pinch of black pepper to make the other spices come through a little bit more. For even more spice, toss in some finely chopped candied ginger after churning. Good on its own, this frozen yogurt is also especially delicious served with a piece of warm gingerbread or spice cake.

1 Bring the milk, molasses, brown sugar, ginger, cinnamon, and pepper to a simmer in a small saucepan over medium heat. Cook, stirring, until the sugar has dissolved. When the mixture comes to a boil, remove from the heat and allow to cool to room temperature.

2 Strain the milk mixture into a small bowl and set aside.

3 Combine the water and granulated sugar in a small saucepan and bring to a boil, without stirring, over medium-high heat. When the sugar mixture comes to a full boil, continue to boil for 1 minute.

4 While the sugar boils, beat the egg whites to soft peaks in a large clean bowl. When the sugar is ready, continue beating the eggs on low speed and very slowly stream in the hot sugar mixture. When all the sugar has been incorporated, turn the mixer to high and beat until the meringue is glossy and has cooled almost down to room temperature, 2 to 3 minutes. (See The Meringue Method, page 10.)

5 Whisk together the yogurt, vanilla, and spiced milk in a large bowl until smooth. Fold in the meringue.

6 Pour the yogurt mixture into an ice cream maker and freeze according to the manufacturer's directions.

7 When the yogurt has finished churning and is still soft, transfer to a large bowl. Fold in the candied ginger, if using, until evenly distributed.

8 Transfer to a freezer-safe container and chill in the freezer for 2 to 3 hours to allow the yogurt to completely set.

Makes about 1½ quarts

- ½ cup whole milk
- ¼ cup unsulfured molasses
- ⅓ cup firmly packed brown sugar
- 2 tablespoons grated fresh ginger
- 1 teaspoon ground cinnamon
- ¼ teaspoon freshly ground black pepper
- ¼ cup water
- ½ cup granulated sugar
- 2 large egg whites, room temperature
- 2 cups plain Greek-style yogurt, cold
- 1 teaspoon vanilla extract
- ⅓ cup finely chopped candied ginger (optional)

TREAT TO TRY

FROZEN PUMPKIN PIE
TERRINE **PAGE 134**

4 CHOCOLATE AND NUTS

Chocolate and yogurt are a surprisingly good combination, and these recipes include milk, dark, and even white chocolate. Chocolate is often, though not always, paired with nuts because the crunch of the nuts complements the creaminess of the chocolate. Frozen yogurt is no exception to this rule, and you'll find many ways to get both chocolate and nut fixes here.

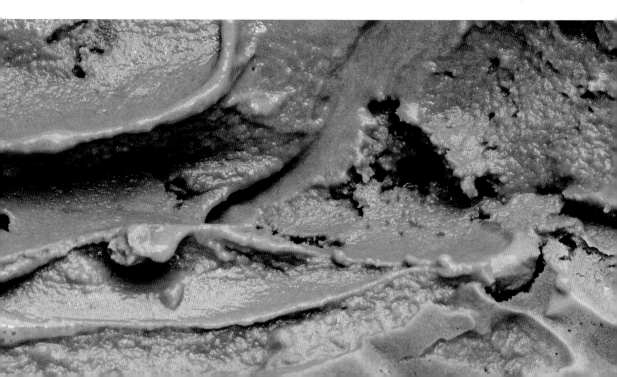

Crème-filled chocolate sandwich cookies, such as Oreos, have such a great flavor that they are often featured in other sweets — like cookies 'n' cream ice cream, a perennial favorite. These delectable cookies work their magic in frozen yogurt just as successfully.

¼ cup water

⅔ cup sugar

2 large egg whites, room temperature

2½ cups plain Greek-style yogurt, cold

2 teaspoons vanilla extract

⅔ cup finely chopped chocolate sandwich cookies, such as Oreos

⅔ cup coarsely chopped chocolate sandwich cookies, such as Oreos

1 Combine the water and sugar in a small saucepan and bring to a boil, without stirring, over medium-high heat. When the sugar mixture comes to a full boil, continue to boil for 1 minute.

2 While the sugar boils, beat the egg whites to soft peaks in a large clean bowl. When the sugar is ready, continue beating the eggs on low speed and very slowly stream in the hot sugar mixture. When all the sugar has been incorporated, turn the mixer to high and beat until the meringue is glossy and has cooled almost down to room temperature, 2 to 3 minutes. (See The Meringue Method, page 10.)

3 Whisk together the yogurt, vanilla, and finely chopped cookies in a large bowl until smooth. Fold in the meringue.

4 Pour the yogurt mixture into an ice cream maker and freeze according to the manufacturer's directions.

5 When the yogurt has finished churning and is still soft, transfer to a large bowl. Fold in the coarsely chopped cookies until evenly distributed.

6 Transfer to a freezer-safe container and chill in the freezer for 2 to 3 hours to allow the yogurt to completely set.

Makes about 2 quarts

TREATS TO TRY

COOKIES 'N' CREAM CAKE
PAGE 110

COOKIE LOVERS' BOMBE
PAGE 138

Chocolate chips are a classic flavor addition to just about any frozen dessert. Store-bought chocolate chips tend to be large and become too hard when frozen, but making your own chips nicely takes care of this. Drizzle melted chocolate into your freshly churned frozen yogurt, and you'll get crisp, easy-to-eat chocolate chips!

1 Combine the water and sugar in a small saucepan and bring to a boil, without stirring, over medium-high heat. When the sugar mixture comes to a full boil, continue to boil for 1 minute.

2 While the sugar boils, beat the egg whites to soft peaks in a large clean bowl. When the sugar is ready, continue beating the eggs on low speed and very slowly stream in the hot sugar mixture. When all the sugar has been incorporated, turn the mixer to high and beat until the meringue is glossy and has cooled almost down to room temperature, 2 to 3 minutes. (See The Meringue Method, page 10.)

3 Whisk together the yogurt and vanilla in a large bowl until smooth. Fold in the meringue.

4 Pour the yogurt mixture into an ice cream maker and freeze according to the manufacturer's directions.

5 When the yogurt has finished churning and is still soft, transfer to a large bowl. Drizzle the melted chocolate over the frozen yogurt while stirring the yogurt with a spatula to create small chocolate "chips" in the yogurt. Stir until all the chocolate has been used and the chips are evenly distributed.

6 Transfer to a freezer-safe container and chill in the freezer for 2 to 3 hours to allow the yogurt to completely set.

Makes about 1½ quarts

¼ cup water

⅔ cup sugar

2 large egg whites, room temperature

2 cups plain Greek-style yogurt, cold

2 teaspoons vanilla extract

4 ounces semisweet or dark chocolate, melted

FLAVOR TWIST

Mint Chocolate Chip: Add 1 teaspoon of peppermint extract to the frozen yogurt base before churning to add a fresh, minty flavor, then proceed with the recipe as directed. If desired, stir in 5 or 6 drops of green food coloring to give this flavor a classic mint-chip look.

ROCKY ROAD

Chocolate goes well with so many flavors, but few combinations are as beloved as rocky road. Chocolate frozen yogurt handles the toasted walnuts and fluffy marshmallows just as well as ice cream does, and the slight tang of the yogurt brings out the sweetness of the marshmallows just a little more than usual.

½ cup whole milk

¼ cup unsweetened cocoa powder

¼ cup water

⅔ cup sugar

2 large egg whites, room temperature

2 cups plain Greek-style yogurt, cold

1 teaspoon vanilla extract

½ cup mini marshmallows

½ cup coarsely chopped toasted walnuts

1 Bring the milk to a simmer in a small saucepan. Add the cocoa powder and stir to dissolve. Set aside to cool slightly.

2 Combine the water and sugar in a small saucepan and bring to a boil, without stirring, over medium-high heat. When the sugar mixture comes to a full boil, continue to boil for 1 minute.

3 While the sugar boils, beat the egg whites to soft peaks in a large clean bowl. When the sugar is ready, continue beating the eggs on low speed and very slowly stream in the hot sugar mixture. When all the sugar has been incorporated, turn the mixer to high and beat until the meringue is glossy and has cooled almost down to room temperature, 2 to 3 minutes. (See The Meringue Method, page 10.)

4 Whisk together the yogurt, vanilla, and cocoa mixture in a large bowl until smooth. Fold in the meringue.

5 Pour the yogurt mixture into an ice cream maker and freeze according to the manufacturer's directions.

6 When the yogurt has finished churning and is still soft, transfer to a large bowl. Fold in the marshmallows and walnuts until evenly distributed.

7 Transfer to a freezer-safe container and chill in the freezer for 2 to 3 hours to allow the yogurt to completely set.

Makes about 1½ quarts

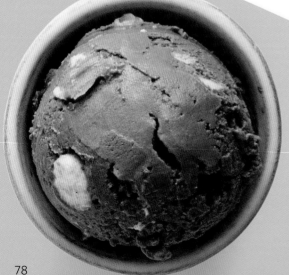

TREAT TO TRY
ROCKY ROAD BROWNIE
SANDWICHES
PAGE 100

There is something irresistible about a buttery, sticky-sweet cookie dough, especially when it's surrounded by vanilla ice cream. This vanilla frozen yogurt might just be a better match for the cookie dough than ice cream. You can make the cookie dough chunks ahead of time and store them in the refrigerator for up to 3 days.

1 Combine the water and granulated sugar in a small saucepan and bring to a boil, without stirring, over medium-high heat. When the sugar mixture comes to a full boil, continue to boil for 1 minute.

2 While the sugar boils, beat the egg whites to soft peaks in a large clean bowl. When the sugar is ready, continue beating the eggs on low speed and very slowly stream in the hot sugar mixture. When all the sugar has been incorporated, turn the mixer to high and beat until the meringue is glossy and has cooled almost down to room temperature, 2 to 3 minutes. (See The Meringue Method, page 10.)

3 Whisk together the yogurt and vanilla in a large bowl until smooth. Fold in the meringue.

4 Pour the yogurt mixture into an ice cream maker and freeze according to the manufacturer's directions.

5 While the yogurt is churning, make the chocolate chip cookie dough chunks: Cream together the butter and brown sugar in a medium bowl. Add the milk, vanilla, and salt, and blend well. Add the flour and mix until the dough comes together. Fold in the chocolate chips. Roll the dough into almond-size balls.

6 When the yogurt has finished churning and is still soft, transfer to a large bowl. Fold in the cookie dough chunks until evenly distributed.

7 Transfer to a freezer-safe container and chill in the freezer for 2 to 3 hours to allow the yogurt to completely set.

Makes about 1½ quarts

¼ cup water

⅔ cup granulated sugar

2 large egg whites, room temperature

2 cups plain Greek-style yogurt, cold

2 teaspoons vanilla extract

CHOCOLATE CHIP COOKIE DOUGH CHUNKS

5 tablespoons plus 1 teaspoon butter, softened

½ cup firmly packed brown sugar

1 tablespoon whole milk

½ teaspoon vanilla extract

¼ teaspoon salt

½ cup unbleached all-purpose flour

½ cup mini chocolate chips

TREAT TO TRY
COOKIE LOVERS' BOMBE
PAGE 138

MOCHA

You don't need to be a barista to know that mochas are popular, hot or cold. Chocolate and coffee are a natural combination, since the two flavors intensify each other.

- ½ cup whole milk
- 3 tablespoons unsweetened cocoa powder
- 1 tablespoon instant coffee or espresso powder
- ¼ cup water
- ⅔ cup sugar
- 2 large egg whites, room temperature
- 2 cups plain Greek-style yogurt, cold
- 2 teaspoons vanilla extract

1 Bring the milk to a simmer in a small saucepan. Add the cocoa powder and coffee powder and stir to dissolve. Set aside to cool slightly.

2 Combine the water and sugar in a small saucepan and bring to a boil, without stirring, over medium-high heat. When the sugar mixture comes to a full boil, continue to boil for 1 minute.

3 While the sugar boils, beat the egg whites to soft peaks in a large clean bowl. When the sugar is ready, continue beating the eggs on low speed and very slowly stream in the hot sugar mixture. When all the sugar has been incorporated, turn the mixer to high and beat until the meringue is glossy and has cooled almost down to room temperature, 2 to 3 minutes. (See The Meringue Method, page 10.)

4 Whisk together the yogurt, vanilla, and milk mixture in a large bowl until smooth. Fold in the meringue.

5 Pour the yogurt mixture into an ice cream maker and freeze according to the manufacturer's directions.

6 Transfer to a freezer-safe container and chill in the freezer for 2 to 3 hours to allow the yogurt to completely set.

Makes about 1½ quarts

FLAVOR TWIST
Mocha Almond Fudge: Add ½ teaspoon of almond extract to the frozen yogurt base before churning. After churning, stir in ¾ cup of chopped toasted almonds and ¾ cup of Chocolate Fudge Sauce (page 162).

Mexican table chocolate is a coarsely textured dark chocolate flavored with spices that often include cinnamon and cayenne, which give a little heat to the chocolate. It's sold in blocks and commonly used to make a spicy — and addictive — hot drink. Those flavors also make a spicy and addictive frozen yogurt.

1 Bring the milk to a simmer in a small saucepan. Combine the chocolate, cocoa powder, cinnamon, and cayenne in a small bowl and pour in the hot milk. Stir to dissolve the chocolate. Set aside to cool to room temperature.

2 Combine the water and sugar in a small saucepan and bring to a boil, without stirring, over medium-high heat. When the sugar mixture comes to a full boil, continue to boil for 1 minute.

3 While the sugar boils, beat the egg whites to soft peaks in a large clean bowl. When the sugar is ready, continue beating the eggs on low speed and very slowly stream in the hot sugar mixture. When all the sugar has been incorporated, turn the mixer to high and beat until the meringue is glossy and has cooled almost down to room temperature, 2 to 3 minutes. (See The Meringue Method, page 10.)

4 Whisk together the yogurt, vanilla, almond extract, and chocolate mixture in a large bowl until smooth. Fold in the meringue.

5 Pour the yogurt mixture into an ice cream maker and freeze according to the manufacturer's directions.

6 Transfer to a freezer-safe container and chill in the freezer for 2 to 3 hours to allow the yogurt to completely set.

Makes about 1½ quarts

- ½ cup whole milk
- 2 ounces Mexican table chocolate or dark chocolate, finely chopped
- 2 tablespoons unsweetened cocoa powder
- ¾ teaspoon ground cinnamon
- ½ teaspoon ground cayenne pepper
- ¼ cup water
- ⅔ cup sugar
- 2 large egg whites, room temperature
- 2 cups plain Greek-style yogurt, cold
- 1 teaspoon vanilla extract
- ¼ teaspoon almond extract

TREAT TO TRY
CHOCOHOLIC COOKIE SANDWICHES
PAGE 99

CHOCOLATE MALTED

A shake made with malted milk powder can take you right back to the days of the old-time soda fountain, and while the powder can be added to all kinds of drinks and baked treats, there is nothing more classic than a chocolate malted. That distinctive malty flavor seems to make the chocolate creamier and the whole thing even more addictive.

½ cup whole milk

⅓ cup malted milk powder

¼ cup unsweetened cocoa powder

¼ cup water

⅔ cup sugar

2 large egg whites, room temperature

2 cups plain Greek-style yogurt, cold

1 teaspoon vanilla extract

FLAVOR TWIST
Malt Ball Chocolate Malted: Stir in 1 cup of crushed chocolate malt ball candies after churning to add more chocolate, malt, and crunch to every scoop.

1 Bring the milk to a simmer in a small saucepan. Add the malted milk powder and cocoa powder and stir to dissolve. Set aside to cool slightly.

2 Combine the water and sugar in a small saucepan and bring to a boil, without stirring, over medium-high heat. When the sugar mixture comes to a full boil, continue to boil for 1 minute.

3 While the sugar boils, beat the egg whites to soft peaks in a large clean bowl. When the sugar is ready, continue beating the eggs on low speed and very slowly stream in the hot sugar mixture. When all the sugar has been incorporated, turn the mixer to high and beat until the meringue is glossy and has cooled almost down to room temperature, 2 to 3 minutes. (See The Meringue Method, page 10.)

4 Whisk together the yogurt, vanilla, and milk mixture in a large bowl until smooth. Fold in the meringue.

5 Pour the yogurt mixture into an ice cream maker and freeze according to the manufacturer's directions.

6 Transfer to a freezer-safe container and chill in the freezer for 2 to 3 hours to allow the yogurt to completely set.

Makes about 1½ quarts

TREATS TO TRY

FLOURLESS PEANUT BUTTER COOKIE SANDWICHES **PAGE 95**

CHOCOLATE MALTED BOMBE **PAGE 140**

White chocolate often gets passed over in favor of more intense dark chocolate, but the vanilla and cream flavors of high-quality white chocolate are a great addition to any frozen dessert. This frozen yogurt also includes sweet-tart raspberries, which add their bright color to the dessert and contrast well with the smooth chocolate base.

1 Combine the water and sugar in a small saucepan and bring to a boil, without stirring, over medium-high heat. When the sugar mixture comes to a full boil, continue to boil for 1 minute.

2 While the sugar boils, beat the egg whites to soft peaks in a large clean bowl. When the sugar is ready, continue beating the eggs on low speed and very slowly stream in the hot sugar mixture. When all the sugar has been incorporated, turn the mixer to high and beat until the meringue is glossy and has cooled almost down to room temperature, 2 to 3 minutes. (See The Meringue Method, page 10.)

3 With the mixer on low, blend the melted chocolate into the meringue.

4 Whisk together the yogurt and vanilla in a large bowl until smooth. Fold in the meringue.

5 Pour the yogurt mixture into an ice cream maker and freeze according to the manufacturer's directions.

6 When the yogurt has finished churning and is still soft, transfer to a large bowl. Fold in the raspberries until evenly distributed.

7 Transfer to a freezer-safe container and chill in the freezer for 2 to 3 hours to allow the yogurt to completely set.

Makes about 1½ quarts

¼ cup water

⅔ cup sugar

2 large egg whites, room temperature

4 ounces white chocolate, melted

2 cups plain Greek-style yogurt, cold

2 teaspoons vanilla extract

¾ cup fresh raspberries

This flavor is inspired by Samoas (also called Caramel deLites, depending on the manufacturer), one of the most popular cookies sold by the Girl Scouts during their annual cookie sale. The frozen yogurt has a vanilla base and is studded with chunks of chocolate-covered shortbread cookie and swirled with a coconut-filled caramel.

¼ cup water

⅔ cup sugar

2 large egg whites, room temperature

2 cups plain Greek-style yogurt, cold

2 teaspoons vanilla extract

3 ounces dark chocolate, chopped

12 shortbread cookies

⅔ cup sweetened shredded coconut

¾ cup caramel sauce, homemade (page 164) or store-bought

1 Combine the water and sugar in a small saucepan and bring to a boil, without stirring, over medium-high heat. When the sugar mixture comes to a full boil, continue to boil for 1 minute.

2 While the sugar boils, beat the egg whites to soft peaks in a large clean bowl. When the sugar is ready, continue beating the eggs on low speed and very slowly stream in the hot sugar mixture. When all the sugar has been incorporated, turn the mixer to high and beat until the meringue is glossy and has cooled almost down to room temperature, 2 to 3 minutes. (See The Meringue Method, page 10.)

3 Whisk together the yogurt and vanilla in a large bowl until smooth. Fold in the meringue.

4 Pour the yogurt mixture into an ice cream maker and freeze according to the manufacturer's directions.

5 While the yogurt is churning, prepare the mix-ins. Melt the dark chocolate in a small microwave-safe bowl in the microwave in 45- to 60-second increments, stirring until smooth. Dip the shortbread cookies into the melted chocolate and place on a sheet of waxed paper. Refrigerate until the chocolate is firm, about 10 minutes. Chop the cookies into chunks.

6 Toast the coconut in a medium skillet over medium heat until golden, stirring frequently, 5 to 7 minutes. Combine the toasted coconut and caramel sauce in a medium bowl.

7 Pour the frozen yogurt into a 9-inch square pan. Drizzle the caramel sauce over it and sprinkle in the chopped cookies. Pull a knife through the frozen yogurt to create a swirl. Freeze for at least 2 to 3 hours to allow the yogurt to completely set before serving.

Makes about 1½ quarts

This is a frozen yogurt for peanut butter lovers, with plenty of peanut butter flavor packed into every bite. Feel free to use crunchy peanut butter if you're after the texture that the peanut bits will give to the yogurt; otherwise, you can opt for the smooth variety.

1 Combine the water and sugar in a small saucepan and bring to a boil, without stirring, over medium-high heat. When the sugar mixture comes to a full boil, continue to boil for 1 minute.

2 While the sugar boils, beat the egg whites to soft peaks in a large clean bowl. When the sugar is ready, continue beating the eggs on low speed and very slowly stream in the hot sugar mixture. When all the sugar has been incorporated, turn the mixer to high and beat until the meringue is glossy and has cooled almost down to room temperature, 2 to 3 minutes. (See The Meringue Method, page 10.)

3 Whisk together the yogurt, peanut butter, vanilla, and salt in a large bowl until smooth. Fold in the meringue.

4 Pour the yogurt mixture into an ice cream maker and freeze according to the manufacturer's directions.

5 Transfer to a freezer-safe container and chill in the freezer for 2 to 3 hours to allow the yogurt to completely set.

Makes about 1½ quarts

¼ cup water

⅔ cup sugar

2 large egg whites, room temperature

2 cups plain Greek-style yogurt, cold

⅔ cup peanut butter, crunchy or smooth

½ teaspoon vanilla extract

¼ teaspoon salt

FLAVOR TWIST
Peanut Butter and Jelly:
For PB&J lovers, gently stir in ½ cup of Easy Strawberry Sauce (page 166) after churning to create a strawberry swirl.

TREATS TO TRY

FLOURLESS PEANUT BUTTER COOKIE SANDWICHES
PAGE 95

PEANUT BUTTER CUP PIE
PAGE 121

CHOCOLATE PB BANANA BOMBE **PAGE 139**

PEANUT BUTTER & MILK CHOCOLATE BONBONS
PAGE 154

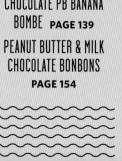

ELVIS

It's on record that Elvis's favorite sandwich was grilled peanut butter and banana (sometimes with honey, and sometimes even with bacon!). Delicious in a hot, toasted sandwich, those ingredients in this frozen yogurt produce a creamy, savory-sweet sensation in every spoonful that's sure to win many fans.

1 large ripe banana

¼ cup water

½ cup sugar

2 large egg whites, room temperature

2 cups plain Greek-style yogurt, cold

⅔ cup peanut butter, crunchy or smooth

⅓ cup honey

½ teaspoon vanilla extract

¼ teaspoon salt

1 Cut the banana into small pieces. Spread in an even layer on a plate or baking dish and place in the freezer to chill.

2 Combine the water and sugar in a small saucepan and bring to a boil, without stirring, over medium-high heat. When the sugar mixture comes to a full boil, continue to boil for 1 minute.

3 While the sugar boils, beat the egg whites to soft peaks in a large clean bowl. When the sugar is ready, continue beating the eggs on low speed and very slowly stream in the hot sugar mixture. When all the sugar has been incorporated, turn the mixer to high and beat until the meringue is glossy and has cooled almost down to room temperature, 2 to 3 minutes. (See The Meringue Method, page 10.)

4 Beat together the yogurt, peanut butter, honey, vanilla, and salt in a large bowl until smooth. Fold in the meringue.

5 Pour the yogurt mixture into an ice cream maker and freeze according to the manufacturer's directions.

6 When the yogurt has finished churning and is still soft, transfer to a large bowl. Fold in the chilled banana pieces until evenly distributed.

7 Transfer to a freezer-safe container and chill in the freezer for 2 to 3 hours to allow the yogurt to completely set.

Makes about 1½ quarts

Nutella is a delicious and hard-to-resist chocolate-hazelnut spread that is popular worldwide. It's enjoyed as a spread on toast for breakfast and in a wide variety of desserts. A generous dose of Nutella gives this milk chocolate–infused frozen yogurt an extra boost of chocolate and a distinctive nutty flavor instantly recognizable to Nutella fans.

1 Combine the milk and chocolate in a small saucepan and cook over low heat, stirring constantly, until the chocolate is fully melted and incorporated. Set aside to cool to room temperature.

2 Combine the water and sugar in a small saucepan and bring to a boil, without stirring, over medium-high heat. When the sugar mixture comes to a full boil, continue to boil for 1 minute.

3 While the sugar boils, beat the egg whites to soft peaks in a large clean bowl. When the sugar is ready, continue beating the eggs on low speed and very slowly stream in the hot sugar mixture. When all the sugar has been incorporated, turn the mixer to high and beat until the meringue is glossy and has cooled almost down to room temperature, 2 to 3 minutes. (See The Meringue Method, page 10.)

4 Beat together the yogurt, Nutella, vanilla, and chocolate milk in a large bowl until smooth. Fold in the meringue.

5 Pour the yogurt mixture into an ice cream maker and freeze according to the manufacturer's directions.

6 Transfer to a freezer-safe container and chill in the freezer for 2 to 3 hours to allow the yogurt to completely set.

Makes about 1½ quarts

- ½ cup whole milk
- 2 ounces milk chocolate, finely chopped
- ¼ cup water
- ⅔ cup sugar
- 2 large egg whites, room temperature
- 2 cups plain Greek-style yogurt, cold
- ½ cup Nutella
- 1 teaspoon vanilla extract

TREAT TO TRY
FROZEN NUTELLA BONBONS **PAGE 150**

PISTACHIO

Pistachios are notable for their beautiful green color, which is a bit trickier to capture than their subtle flavor. This recipe gives your yogurt a tint of color and bright dots of crunchy chopped nuts, but you can add a few drops of green food coloring to the base if you like. *Note:* Step 1 is simple, but it does need to be done several hours or the day before completing the recipe.

⅔ cup heavy cream

⅔ cup raw pistachios, finely chopped

¼ cup water

⅔ cup sugar

2 large egg whites, room temperature

2 cups plain Greek-style yogurt, cold

1 teaspoon vanilla extract

⅔ cup coarsely chopped raw or toasted pistachios

1 Bring the cream to a boil in a small saucepan over medium-high heat. Place the raw pistachios in a small bowl and pour in the hot cream. Cover and allow the pistachios to steep for several hours, or overnight in the refrigerator. Strain the cream into a small bowl and discard the pistachios.

2 Combine the water and sugar in a small saucepan and bring to a boil, without stirring, over medium-high heat. When the sugar mixture comes to a full boil, continue to boil for 1 minute.

3 While the sugar boils, beat the egg whites to soft peaks in a large clean bowl. When the sugar is ready, continue beating the eggs on low speed and very slowly stream in the hot sugar mixture. When all the sugar has been incorporated, turn the mixer to high and beat until the meringue is glossy and has cooled almost down to room temperature, 2 to 3 minutes. (See The Meringue Method, page 10.)

4 Whisk together the yogurt, vanilla, and pistachio cream in a large bowl until smooth. Fold in the meringue.

5 Pour the yogurt mixture into an ice cream maker and freeze according to the manufacturer's directions.

6 When the yogurt has finished churning and is still soft, transfer to a large bowl. Fold in the coarsely chopped pistachios until evenly distributed.

7 Transfer to a freezer-safe container and chill in the freezer for 2 to 3 hours to allow the yogurt to completely set.

Makes about 1½ quarts

TREAT TO TRY
SPUMONI TERRINE
PAGE 131

Amaretto is an almond liqueur with an intense flavor that gives a lot of character to this frozen yogurt. The almond flavor is heightened by the addition of finely chopped toasted almonds, which also give a nice little crunch. Sprinkling the almonds with salt just after toasting lends a hint of savoriness and really brings out their flavor.

1 Preheat the oven to 350°F/180°C. Spread the almonds on a baking sheet and toast, stirring occasionally, for 5 to 10 minutes, until golden. Sprinkle with the salt. Set aside to cool completely.

2 Combine the water and sugar in a small saucepan and bring to a boil, without stirring, over medium-high heat. When the sugar mixture comes to a full boil, continue to boil for 1 minute.

3 While the sugar boils, beat the egg whites to soft peaks in a large clean bowl. When the sugar is ready, continue beating the eggs on low speed and very slowly stream in the hot sugar mixture. When all the sugar has been incorporated, turn the mixer to high and beat until the meringue is glossy and has cooled almost down to room temperature, 2 to 3 minutes. (See The Meringue Method, page 10.)

4 Whisk together the yogurt, vanilla, and amaretto in a large bowl until smooth. Fold in the meringue.

5 Pour the yogurt mixture into an ice cream maker and freeze according to the manufacturer's directions.

6 When the yogurt has finished churning and is still soft, transfer to a large bowl. Fold in the toasted almonds until evenly distributed.

7 Transfer to a freezer-safe container and chill in the freezer for 2 to 3 hours to allow the yogurt to completely set.

Makes about 1½ quarts

1 cup finely chopped unsalted almonds

¼ teaspoon salt

¼ cup water

⅔ cup sugar

2 large egg whites, room temperature

2 cups plain Greek-style yogurt, cold

1 teaspoon vanilla extract

3 tablespoons amaretto

TREAT TO TRY
BUTTERSCOTCH ALMOND TORTE PAGE 114

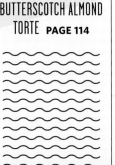

BROWNED BUTTER PECAN

The only way to make browned butter even more delicious is by adding pecans to it, and the only way to top that is to make butter pecan frozen yogurt. In this recipe, toasted pecans are coated with browned butter and then added to a nutty, brown butter–infused yogurt for a dessert that gives stiff competition to its ice cream counterpart.

- 6 tablespoons butter
- 1 cup finely chopped pecans
- ¼ cup water
- ⅔ cup sugar
- 2 large egg whites, room temperature
- 2 cups plain Greek-style yogurt, cold
- 2 teaspoons vanilla extract

1 Place the butter in a small saucepan and melt, without stirring, over medium heat until the butter bubbles and foams, 3 to 4 minutes. When the foam has subsided, it will begin to brown and release a nutty smell. Stir the butter with a spatula as it browns to prevent burning, scraping the brown bits off the bottom of the pan. Cook and stir until the butter is golden brown, 1 to 3 minutes. Transfer to a small bowl and set aside to cool to room temperature.

2 Preheat the oven to 350°F/180°C. Spread the pecans on a baking sheet and toast, stirring occasionally, for 5 to 10 minutes, until golden. Transfer the pecans to a small bowl and toss with 2 tablespoons of the browned butter. Return the pecans to the baking sheet to cool.

3 Combine the water and sugar in a small saucepan and bring to a boil, without stirring, over medium-high heat. When the sugar mixture comes to a full boil, continue to boil for 1 minute.

4 While the sugar boils, beat the egg whites to soft peaks in a large clean bowl. When the sugar is ready, continue beating the eggs on low speed and very slowly stream in the hot sugar mixture. When all the sugar has been incorporated, turn the mixer to high and beat until the meringue is glossy and has cooled almost down to room temperature, 2 to 3 minutes. (See The Meringue Method, page 10.)

TREAT TO TRY
BUTTER PECAN PIE
PAGE 122

5 Fold the remaining browned butter into about 1 cup of the meringue in a small bowl until incorporated.

6 Whisk together the yogurt and vanilla in a large bowl until smooth. Fold in the plain meringue and the browned butter meringue.

7 Pour the yogurt mixture into an ice cream maker and freeze according to the manufacturer's directions.

8 When the yogurt has finished churning and is still soft, transfer to a large bowl. Fold in the buttered pecans until evenly distributed.

9 Transfer to a freezer-safe container and chill in the freezer for 2 to 3 hours to allow the yogurt to completely set.

Makes about 1½ quarts

COOKIE AND BROWNIE SANDWICHES

5

When you add a frozen filling, you can turn a good cookie into a very memorable dessert. Almost any filling can be used with these delicious cookie recipes, so use the suggested frozen yogurt filling flavors just as a guideline to get started.

It is hard to go wrong with a classic chocolate chip cookie, and the same holds true for a chocolate chip cookie sandwich. These buttery cookies are loaded with chocolate chips and have a tender chewy texture that makes them easy to bite into, even after they have been frozen. I typically pair them with chocolate chip frozen yogurt, but they're versatile enough to work with any flavor.

2½ cups unbleached all-purpose flour

1 teaspoon baking soda

1 teaspoon salt

1 cup (2 sticks) butter, softened

1 cup granulated sugar

½ cup firmly packed dark brown sugar

2 large eggs

2 teaspoons vanilla extract

2 cups chocolate chips

Chocolate Chip frozen yogurt (page 77), slightly softened, for filling

1 Preheat the oven to 375°F/190°C. Line a baking sheet with parchment paper.

2 Whisk together the flour, baking soda, and salt in a medium bowl.

3 Cream together the butter and granulated and brown sugars in a large bowl until light and creamy. Beat in the eggs one at a time, then add the vanilla. Gradually blend in the flour mixture, then stir in the chocolate chips.

4 Shape the dough into 1-inch balls and arrange the balls on the prepared baking sheet, leaving about 2 inches between the cookies to allow them to spread.

5 Bake for 11 to 13 minutes, until the cookies are light golden around the edges. Let the cookies cool on the baking sheet for 5 minutes, then transfer them to a wire rack to cool completely.

6 Fill the cooled cookies with frozen yogurt, then freeze until ready to serve. The sandwiches can be individually wrapped and stored in the freezer for several weeks.

Makes about 40 cookies or 20 frozen yogurt sandwiches

Cookies don't get much easier to make than this flourless peanut butter cookie recipe. These gluten-free cookies have a chewy texture and a great peanut butter flavor. I usually serve them with chocolate or peanut butter frozen yogurt, but you could use a fruity filling for a twist on classic peanut butter and jelly, too.

1 Preheat the oven to 350°F/180°C. Line a baking sheet with parchment paper.

2 Combine the peanut butter and sugar in a large bowl and beat until light and creamy. Beat in the eggs, vanilla, baking soda, and salt until the dough is uniform.

3 Shape the dough into 1-inch balls and arrange the balls on the prepared baking sheet, leaving about 2 inches between cookies to allow for spread. Flatten slightly with a fork.

4 Bake for 10 to 13 minutes, until the cookies are golden brown at the edges. Let the cookies cool on the baking sheet for 5 minutes, then transfer them to a wire rack to cool completely.

5 Fill the cooled cookies with frozen yogurt. Place the chopped nuts in a shallow bowl and roll the edge of the sandwiches in the nuts. Freeze until firm before serving. The sandwiches can be individually wrapped and stored in the freezer for several weeks.

Makes about 48 cookies or 24 frozen yogurt sandwiches

2 cups smooth peanut butter

1½ cups firmly packed light brown sugar

2 large eggs

1 teaspoon vanilla extract

1 teaspoon baking soda

¼ teaspoon salt

Chocolate Malted frozen yogurt (page 82), Peanut Butter frozen yogurt (page 85), or Fresh Strawberry frozen yogurt (page 37), slightly softened, for filling

1 cup chopped roasted salted peanuts

Frozen cookie sandwiches don't always involve fruit, but a fruity filling pairs very well with these classic sugar cookies. They are a great choice for summer entertaining. That said, you can easily make them seasonal by switching up the filling. Try using dried cranberries in the cookies and pair them with Cranberry frozen yogurt (page 42), or opt for Peach Melba frozen yogurt (page 44) and skip the dried fruit entirely.

1 Preheat the oven to 350°F/180°C. Line a baking sheet with parchment paper.

2 Whisk together the flour, baking soda, and salt in a medium bowl.

3 Cream together the butter and 1½ cups of the sugar in a large bowl until light and fluffy. Add the eggs and vanilla and beat until well combined. With the mixer on low speed, gradually incorporate the flour mixture until the dough comes together and no streaks of dry ingredients remain. Stir in the dried blueberries.

4 Place the remaining ½ cup sugar in a small shallow bowl. Shape the dough into 1-inch balls, roll in the sugar, and place on the prepared baking sheet. Leave about 2 inches between cookies to allow for spread.

5 Bake for 11 to 13 minutes, until the cookies are set and very light golden around the edges. Let the cookies cool on the baking sheet for 3 to 4 minutes, then transfer them to a wire rack to cool completely.

6 Fill the cooled cookies with frozen yogurt. Freeze until firm before serving. The sandwiches can be individually wrapped and stored in the freezer for several weeks.

Makes about 40 cookies or 20 frozen yogurt sandwiches

2¼ cups unbleached all-purpose flour

1 teaspoon baking soda

½ teaspoon salt

¾ cup (1½ sticks) butter, softened

2 cups sugar

2 large eggs

1 teaspoon vanilla extract

⅔ cup dried blueberries

Double Blueberry frozen yogurt (page 30), slightly softened, for filling

Gingersnaps are one of my favorite cookies to pair with frozen yogurt because the spicy cookies provide such a wonderful contrast to simple flavors like vanilla and chocolate. While you could simply stick a cookie into a scoop of ice cream, they're even better when served as frozen yogurt–filled sandwiches.

2 cups unbleached all-purpose flour

2 tablespoons cornstarch

2 teaspoons baking soda

¼ teaspoon salt

2 teaspoons ground ginger

1 teaspoon ground cinnamon

¼ teaspoon ground cloves

¼ teaspoon freshly ground black pepper

1⅔ cups sugar

⅔ cup vegetable oil

⅓ cup molasses

1 teaspoon vanilla extract

Ginger & Cardamom frozen yogurt (page 54) or Cookie Butter frozen yogurt (page 60), slightly softened, for filling

1 Preheat the oven to 350°F/180°C. Line a baking sheet with parchment paper.

2 Whisk together the flour, cornstarch, baking soda, salt, ginger, cinnamon, cloves, and pepper in a large bowl.

3 Whisk together 1 cup of the sugar, the oil, the molasses, and the vanilla in a medium bowl. Pour into the flour mixture and stir until no streaks of dry ingredients remain.

4 Place the remaining ⅔ cup sugar in a shallow bowl. Shape the dough into 1-inch balls, roll in the sugar, and place on the prepared baking sheet. Leave about 2 inches between cookies to allow for spread.

5 Bake for 7 to 9 minutes, until the outside edges of the cookies are set. Do not overbake. Let the cookies cool on the baking sheet for 3 to 5 minutes, then transfer them to a wire rack to cool completely.

6 Fill the cooled cookies with frozen yogurt. Freeze until firm before serving. The sandwiches can be individually wrapped and stored in the freezer for several weeks.

Makes about 36 cookies or 18 frozen yogurt sandwiches

Only for chocolate lovers, these chocolate cookies are studded with three types of chocolate and sandwiched together with chocolate frozen yogurt. I usually stick with classic Chocolate frozen yogurt for these sandwiches, but Dark Chocolate and Mexican Spiced Hot Chocolate are also excellent flavors to try.

1 Preheat the oven to 350°F/180°C. Line a baking sheet with parchment paper.

2 Sift together the flour, cocoa powder, baking soda, and salt in a medium bowl.

3 Cream together the butter and sugar in a large bowl until light and fluffy. Beat in the eggs one at a time, then add the vanilla and mix until smooth. With the mixer on low speed, gradually incorporate the flour mixture into the butter mixture until well combined and no streaks of flour remain. Stir in the dark chocolate chunks and mik and white chocolate chips.

4 Shape the dough into 1-inch balls and arrange on the prepared baking sheet, leaving about 2 inches between the cookies to allow for spread.

5 Bake for 11 to 12 minutes, until the cookies are set around the edges. Let the cookies cool on the baking sheet for 4 to 5 minutes, then transfer them to a wire rack to cool completely.

6 Fill the cooled cookies with frozen yogurt. Freeze until firm before serving. The sandwiches can be individually wrapped and stored in the freezer for several weeks.

Makes about 48 cookies or 24 frozen yogurt sandwiches

2 cups unbleached all-purpose flour

⅔ cup unsweetened cocoa powder

½ teaspoon baking soda

½ teaspoon salt

1 cup (2 sticks) butter, softened

1½ cups sugar

2 large eggs

1 teaspoon vanilla extract

1 cup dark chocolate chunks

½ cup milk chocolate chips

½ cup white chocolate chips

Chocolate frozen yogurt (page 25), Dark Chocolate frozen yogurt (page 26), or Mexican Spiced Hot Chocolate frozen yogurt (page 81), slightly softened, for filling

Chocolate and vanilla may be a classic ice cream sandwich combination, but there is nothing wrong with a little extra chocolate, either! These rich, fudgy brownies are sandwiched together with my wonderful Rocky Road frozen yogurt.

¾ cup (1½ sticks) butter

¾ cup unsweetened cocoa powder

1½ cups sugar

3 large eggs

1 teaspoon vanilla extract

1½ cups unbleached all-purpose flour

¼ teaspoon salt

Rocky Road frozen yogurt (page 78), slightly softened, for filling

1 Preheat the oven to 350°F/180°C. Line a 9- by 13-inch baking dish with aluminum foil, allowing the foil to hang over the edges, and lightly grease the foil.

2 Melt the butter in a medium microwave-safe bowl in the microwave. Add the cocoa powder to the butter and whisk until well combined. Allow to cool slightly.

3 Combine the sugar and eggs in a large bowl and whisk until the mixture is smooth. Whisk in the butter mixture, followed by the vanilla.

4 Stir in the flour and salt and mix until everything is just combined and no streaks of dry ingredients remain. Pour the batter into the prepared pan.

5 Bake for 20 to 25 minutes, until the brownies are set and a toothpick inserted into the center comes out with only a few moist crumbs attached. Let the brownies cool completely in the pan.

6 When the brownies are cool, use the foil to lift the sheet of brownies out of the pan and place them on a cutting board. Cut the brownies lengthwise down the center, creating two long strips of brownie (4½ by 13 inches). Use a spatula to loosen the brownies from the foil and set one strip aside.

7 Transfer the second brownie strip to a large clean piece of foil. Spread the frozen yogurt over the strip of brownie, creating a thick and even layer. Place the second brownie strip on top and gently press into place. Wrap up the brownie log in the foil and transfer to the freezer to set up, at least 3 to 4 hours.

8 When ready to serve, cut the brownies into individual sandwiches (1 by 4½ inches). The sandwiches can be individually wrapped and stored in the freezer for several weeks.

Makes 12 frozen yogurt sandwiches

Buttery blondies surround a decadent strawberry cheesecake filling that makes these sandwiches feel particularly indulgent. For a little extra strawberry flavor, pick up some freeze-dried strawberries and stir them into the blondie batter. They'll add an extra pop of color to the blondie bars and another layer of strawberry flavor.

1 Preheat the oven to 350°F/180°C. Line a 9- by 13-inch baking dish with aluminum foil, allowing the foil to hang over the edges, and lightly grease the foil.

2 Melt the butter in a medium microwave-safe bowl in the microwave. Allow to cool slightly.

3 Whisk together the sugar, eggs, and egg yolk in a large bowl until the mixture is smooth. Whisk in the butter, followed by the vanilla.

4 Whisk together the flour, baking soda, and salt in a medium bowl. Pour the dry ingredients into the bowl with the butter mixture and stir until everything is just combined and no streaks of dry ingredients remain. Fold in the freeze-dried strawberries, if using. Pour the batter into the prepared pan.

5 Bake for 25 to 28 minutes, until the blondies are set and a toothpick inserted into the center comes out with only a few moist crumbs attached. Let the blondies cool completely in the pan.

6 When the blondies are cool, use the foil to lift the sheet of blondies out of the pan and place them on a cutting board. Cut the blondies lengthwise down the center, creating two long strips of cookie (4½ by 13 inches). Use a spatula to loosen the blondies from the foil and set one strip aside.

7 Transfer one blondie strip to a large clean piece of foil. Spread the frozen yogurt over the strip of blondie, creating a thick and even layer. Place the second blondie strip on top and gently press into place. Wrap up the blondie log in the foil and transfer to the freezer to set up, at least 3 to 4 hours.

8 When ready to serve, cut the blondies into individual sandwiches (1 by 4½ inches). The sandwiches can be individually wrapped and stored in the freezer for several weeks.

Makes 12 frozen yogurt sandwiches

¾ cup (1½ sticks) butter, softened

1½ cups sugar

2 large eggs

1 large egg yolk

2 teaspoons vanilla extract

2 cups unbleached all-purpose flour

½ teaspoon baking soda

½ teaspoon salt

½ cup freeze-dried strawberries (optional)

Strawberry Cheesecake frozen yogurt (page 38), slightly softened, for filling

Ice cream sandwiches may be more popular during the summer than they are during the colder months, but these festive brownie sandwiches are perfect for pairing with a mug of hot chocolate during the winter.

1 Preheat the oven to 350°F/180°C. Line a 9- by 13-inch baking dish with aluminum foil, letting the foil overhang the edges, and lightly grease the foil.

2 Melt the butter in a medium microwave-safe bowl in the microwave. Add the cocoa powder and whisk until well combined. Allow to cool slightly.

3 Whisk together the sugar and eggs in a large bowl until the mixture is smooth. Whisk in the butter mixture, followed by the vanilla and the peppermint extract.

4 Stir in the flour and salt until everything is just combined and no streaks of dry ingredients remain. Fold in the chocolate chips. Pour the batter into the prepared pan. Sprinkle the peppermint candies over the top of the brownies.

5 Bake for 20 to 25 minutes, until the brownies are set and a toothpick inserted into the center comes out with only a few moist crumbs attached. Let the brownies cool completely in the pan.

6 When the brownies are cool, use the foil to lift the sheet of brownies out of the pan and place them on a cutting board. Cut the brownies lengthwise down the center, creating two long strips of brownie (4½ by 13 inches). Use a spatula to loosen the brownies from the foil and set one piece aside.

7 Transfer the second brownie strip to a large clean piece of foil, peppermint side down. Spread the frozen yogurt over the strip of brownie, creating a thick and even layer. Place the second brownie strip on top, peppermint side up, and gently press into place. Wrap up the brownie log in the foil and transfer to the freezer to set up, at least 3 to 4 hours.

8 When ready to serve, cut the brownies into individual sandwiches (1 by 4½ inches). The sandwiches can be individually wrapped and stored in the freezer for several weeks.

Makes 12 frozen yogurt sandwiches

¾ cup (1½ sticks) butter

¾ cup unsweetened cocoa powder

1½ cups sugar

3 large eggs

1 teaspoon vanilla extract

½ teaspoon peppermint extract

1½ cups unbleached all-purpose flour

¼ teaspoon salt

½ cup white chocolate chips

⅓ cup crushed peppermint candies

Candy Cane frozen yogurt (page 71), slightly softened, for filling

CAKES, CUPCAKES, AND PIES

6

Frozen cakes and pies are always a welcome addition to a celebration, whether you're having a birthday party or a holiday gathering. Not only are they delicious, but they can and should be prepared in advance, which means that you don't need to spend time prepping the cake before you intend to serve it. Leftovers can be stored in the freezer for late-night snacking, too.

This towering layer cake was inspired by a traditional banana split, though this format is far from traditional!

1 Line three 9-inch round cake pans with plastic wrap. Spoon one flavor of frozen yogurt into each of the pans and press into an even layer. Freeze until firm, at least 1 hour.

2 Preheat the oven to 350°F/180°C. Grease a 9-inch round cake pan and line the bottom with a circle of parchment paper.

3 Make the brownie base: Melt together the chocolate and butter in a small microwave-safe bowl in the microwave. Heat in 30- to 60-second increments and stir well after each to avoid burning the mixture. Let cool for 5 to 8 minutes.

4 Pour the butter mixture into a large bowl and add the granulated sugar. Whisk in the eggs one at a time, followed by the vanilla. Stir in the flour and salt, mixing until no streaks of dry ingredients remain. Pour the batter into the prepared pan.

5 Bake for 38 to 40 minutes, until a toothpick inserted into the center comes out almost clean, with a few crumbs attached. Let the brownie base cool for 5 minutes in the pan, then invert onto a cooling rack and cool completely. Freeze the brownie base for about 30 minutes, until firm.

6 Remove the brownie base from the freezer and, using a serrated knife, cut the cake into two layers. Place one brownie layer cut-side up on a serving platter. Top with the banana frozen yogurt layer, the strawberry frozen yogurt layer, and the chocolate frozen yogurt layer. Place the second brownie layer on top, cut-side down. Chill the cake in the freezer.

7 For the topping, beat the cream to soft peaks in a large bowl. Beat in the confectioners' sugar and vanilla. Remove the cake from the freezer and spread a thin layer of whipped cream over the whole cake, using an offset spatula to smooth the top and sides. Freeze for 20 minutes.

8 Warm the chocolate fudge sauce slightly until thick but pourable. Drizzle over the top of the cake and garnish the cake with the cherries. Freeze until ready to serve.

Serves 10

1 batch Roasted Banana & Salted Caramel frozen yogurt (page 48), slightly softened

1 batch Fresh Strawberry frozen yogurt (page 37), slightly softened

1 batch Chocolate frozen yogurt (page 25), slightly softened

BROWNIE BASE

5 ounces dark chocolate, finely chopped

¾ cup (1½ sticks) butter

1 cup granulated sugar

3 large eggs

1 teaspoon vanilla extract

⅓ cup unbleached all-purpose flour

¼ teaspoon salt

TOPPINGS

3 cups heavy cream

1 cup confectioners' sugar

2 teaspoons vanilla extract

1 cup Chocolate Fudge Sauce (page 162)

10 maraschino cherries

To cut horizontally, use a long serrated knife and hold it against the side of the brownie layer. Rotate the brownie while pressing the knife firmly into the brownie to get an even cut all the way through.

This layered cake is like a mocha latte in frozen form, and it packs a caffeine punch in every piece. With layers of chocolate, coffee, and vanilla, it is a showstopper, too.

BROWNIE BASE

- 5 ounces dark chocolate, finely chopped
- ¾ cup (1½ sticks) butter
- 1 cup granulated sugar
- 3 large eggs
- 1 teaspoon vanilla extract
- ⅓ cup unbleached all-purpose flour
- ¼ teaspoon salt

- 1 batch Coffee frozen yogurt (page 27), slightly softened
- 1 cup heavy cream
- ⅓ cup confectioners' sugar
- 2 tablespoons unsweetened cocoa powder, plus more for dusting
- 1 teaspoon vanilla extract
- ¼ cup chocolate-covered coffee beans

1 Preheat the oven to 350°F/180°C. Grease a 9-inch round cake pan and line the bottom with a circle of parchment paper.

2 Make the brownie base: Melt together the chocolate and butter in a small microwave-safe bowl in the microwave. Heat in 30- to 60-second increments and stir well after each to avoid burning the mixture. Let cool for 5 to 8 minutes.

3 Pour the butter mixture into a large bowl and add the granulated sugar. Whisk in the eggs one at a time, followed by the vanilla. Stir in the flour and salt, mixing until no streaks of dry ingredients remain. Pour the batter into the prepared pan.

4 Bake for 38 to 40 minutes, until a toothpick inserted into the center comes out almost clean, with a few crumbs attached. Let the brownie base cool for 5 minutes in the pan, then invert onto a cooling rack and cool completely. Freeze the brownie base for about 30 minutes, until firm.

5 Place the cooled brownie base in a 9-inch springform pan. Spoon the frozen yogurt over the top of the brownie base, spreading it into an even layer. Freeze until firm, at least 30 minutes.

6 While the frozen yogurt is freezing, beat the cream to soft peaks in a large bowl. Sift in the confectioners' sugar and cocoa powder and beat until completely incorporated. Blend in the vanilla.

7 Spoon the whipped cream on top of the coffee frozen yogurt and spread into an even layer. Garnish with a ring of chocolate-covered coffee beans around the top edge of the cake. Freeze until completely set, at least 2 hours.

8 To unmold, release the sides of the springform pan and slide the cake onto a serving platter. Dust with additional cocoa powder before slicing.

Serves 8-10

While most ice cream cakes are made with layers of ice cream, this one has an ice cream filling that is surrounded by chocolate cake on all sides. The assembly is a little bit more complicated than some of those other cakes, but the impressive (and delicious) results are well worth the effort.

½ cup unbleached all-purpose flour

⅓ cup unsweetened cocoa powder

½ teaspoon baking powder

¼ teaspoon baking soda

⅛ teaspoon salt

4 large eggs, separated

½ plus ⅓ cup sugar

⅓ cup water

1 teaspoon vanilla extract

1 batch Cookies 'n' Cream frozen yogurt (page 76), slightly softened

½ cup heavy cream

4 ounces dark chocolate, finely chopped

4 ounces milk chocolate, finely chopped

½ cup coarsely chopped chocolate sandwich cookies, such as Oreos

1 Preheat the oven to 375°F/190°C. Lightly grease a 10- by 15-inch jelly-roll pan and line the bottom with parchment paper.

2 Sift together the flour, cocoa powder, baking powder, baking soda, and salt in a medium bowl.

3 Beat the egg yolks and ⅓ cup of the sugar in a large bowl until the sugar is dissolved and the mixture has doubled in volume. Stir in one-third of the flour mixture, followed by half of the water and the vanilla. Stir in another third of the flour mixture, followed by the rest of the water and then the remaining flour mixture.

4 Beat the egg whites in another large bowl until they reach soft peaks. With the mixer on high, gradually blend in the remaining ½ cup sugar, beating until all the sugar is dissolved. Fold the egg whites into the chocolate mixture.

5 Pour the cake batter into the prepared pan and spread into an even layer.

6 Bake for 11 to 15 minutes, until the cake springs back when lightly pressed. Turn the cake out onto a wire rack to cool completely.

7 Line a 5- by 9-inch loaf pan with plastic wrap.

8 Cut pieces of the cake to fit the bottom, sides, and top of the loaf pan. Place the bottom and side pieces into place. Fill the cake completely with the frozen yogurt and spread gently into an even layer. Place the top piece of cake into place, wrap the pan firmly in plastic wrap, and freeze until solid, at least 6 hours.

9 When the cake is completely frozen, prepare a ganache glaze: Bring the cream to a simmer in a small saucepan. Combine the dark and milk chocolates in a medium bowl. Pour the simmering cream over the chocolate and stir gently with a spatula until the chocolate melts and the mixture is smooth. Allow the ganache to cool and thicken slightly, 10 to 15 minutes.

10 Remove the cake from the pan and invert onto a serving platter. Pour the ganache over the cake, using an offset spatula to spread it into an even layer on the top and sides. Garnish the top of the cake with crushed cookies. The ganache will set up quickly and the cake can be served immediately, or it can be frozen until you're ready to serve.

Serves 10

For those who can't get enough of those cinnamon-kissed sugar cookies, this snickerdoodle-inspired cake is the perfect dessert. Two layers of cinnamon cake sandwich Snickerdoodle frozen yogurt filling, and the whole cake is wrapped in a layer of cinnamon frosting!

1 Preheat the oven to 350°F/180°C. Lightly grease two 9-inch round cake pans and line the bottoms with parchment paper.

2 Whisk together the flour, cinnamon, baking soda, and salt in a medium bowl.

3 Cream together the butter and granulated sugar in a large bowl until light and creamy. Beat in the eggs one at a time, followed by the vanilla. Mix in half of the flour mixture, followed by the milk. Stir in the remaining flour mixture, mixing just until no streaks of dry ingredients remain visible and the batter is uniform. Divide the batter evenly into the prepared cake pans.

4 Bake for 18 to 22 minutes, until a toothpick inserted into the center of the cakes comes out clean and the cakes spring back when lightly pressed.

5 Turn the cakes out onto a wire rack and allow to cool completely.

6 While the cakes are cooling, line a 9-inch round cake pan with plastic wrap. Spoon the frozen yogurt into the pan, spreading it into an even layer. Freeze until firm, at least 60 minutes.

7 While the frozen yogurt is freezing, make the cinnamon buttercream frosting: Cream together the butter, cinnamon, milk, vanilla, and 2 cups of the confectioners' sugar in a large bowl until smooth. Gradually blend in the remaining confectioners' sugar until the frosting is thick and spreadable.

8 To assemble the cake, place one cake on a serving platter or cake tray. Top with the frozen yogurt layer, then place the remaining cake layer on top. If the frozen yogurt is melting, freeze the assembled cake for 30 minutes before frosting. Spread the frosting over the top and sides of the cake before serving. Top with chunks of snickerdoodle cookies, if using.

Serves 10-12

1½ cups unbleached all-purpose flour

2 teaspoons ground cinnamon

¾ teaspoon baking soda

¼ teaspoon salt

½ cup (1 stick) butter, softened

1¼ cups granulated sugar

3 large eggs

½ teaspoon vanilla extract

⅔ cup milk

1 quart Snickerdoodle frozen yogurt (page 69), slightly softened

CINNAMON BUTTERCREAM FROSTING

1 cup (2 sticks) butter, softened

1 teaspoon ground cinnamon

3 tablespoons milk

2 teaspoons vanilla extract

3-4 cups confectioners' sugar

Snickerdoodle cookies, broken into chunks, for garnish (optional)

This simple layered dessert is a riff on a classic strawberry shortcake. Instead of cake, it has a topping made with buttery shortbread cookies and toasted pecans, which add some nice crunch to the two creamy frozen yogurt layers. Spoon some strawberry sauce over the top of each piece before serving.

1 Line a springform pan with plastic wrap. Stir together the cookie crumbs and pecans in a small bowl, then pour into the pan and spread into an even layer. Spoon the strawberry frozen yogurt over the shortbread mixture, gently spreading it until it covers the whole pan. Freeze until firm, about 30 minutes.

2 Spoon the vanilla frozen yogurt over the strawberry layer, spreading it into an even layer. Freeze until very firm, at least 1 hour.

3 Invert the pan onto a serving platter. Remove the sides and bottom of the pan and remove the plastic wrap. Drizzle the strawberry sauce over the top of the torte. Slice with a hot, dry knife.

Serves 8

1 cup shortbread cookie crumbs

¼ cup chopped pecans, toasted

2 cups Fresh Strawberry frozen yogurt (page 37), slightly softened

3 cups Vanilla Bean frozen yogurt (page 23), slightly softened

1 cup Easy Strawberry Sauce (page 166)

STRAWBERRY SHORTCAKE TORTE

This easy-to-make torte is a simple but elegant dessert, thanks in large part to the complexity of the Roasted Almond & Amaretto frozen yogurt that makes up the body of the dish. A layer of toasted almonds adds texture and a pretty finished look, making the torte surprisingly impressive.

½ cup sliced almonds, toasted

1 batch Roasted Almond & Amaretto frozen yogurt (page 89), slightly softened

½ cup Butterscotch Sauce (page 168)

1 Line a springform pan with plastic wrap and cover the base evenly with the almonds. Spoon the frozen yogurt over the sliced almonds, gently spreading it until it covers the whole pan. Freeze until firm, about 1 hour.

2 Invert the pan onto a serving platter. Remove the sides and bottom of the pan and remove the plastic wrap. Heat the butterscotch sauce in a small bowl in the microwave and drizzle over the top of the torte. Slice with a hot, dry knife.

Serves 8

These cupcakes were inspired by a popular snack cake filled with crème and rolled in shredded coconut. The frozen version features vanilla cupcakes filled with coconut frozen yogurt, coated in a thin layer of frosting and a generous finishing layer of coconut.

1 Preheat the oven to 350°F/180°C. Line a 12-cup muffin pan with paper liners.

2 Whisk together the flour, baking powder, and salt in a medium bowl.

3 Cream together the butter and granulated sugar in a large bowl until light and fluffy. Beat in the eggs, one at a time, followed by the oil.

4 Stir half of the dry ingredients into the egg mixture, followed by the buttermilk and vanilla. Stir in the remaining dry ingredients, mixing just until no streaks of flour remain. Divide the batter evenly into the prepared muffin cups.

5 Bake for 15 to 17 minutes, until a toothpick inserted into the center of each cupcake comes out clean and the top springs back when lightly pressed. Let the cupcakes cool completely on a wire rack.

6 Hollow out the cool cupcakes using a cupcake corer or by using a paring knife to carefully remove a wide, cone-shaped core of cupcake from the top. Reserve the top of each core to serve as a "plug" for the cupcake.

7 Fill each cored cupcake with 2 to 3 tablespoons of the frozen yogurt. Place the cake plug over the frozen yogurt to enclose it. Freeze for at least 15 minutes to allow the frozen yogurt to set up before frosting.

8 To prepare the frosting, beat the butter, milk, vanilla, and 2 cups of the confectioners' sugar together in a large bowl until very smooth. Gradually blend in the remaining confectioners' sugar until the frosting is thick, smooth, and spreadable.

9 Place the shredded coconut in a shallow bowl or plate. If you would like to make pink coconut, stir in 4 or 5 drops of food coloring to tint it.

10 Remove the cupcakes from the freezer. For each one, spread a thin layer of frosting over the whole cupcake and then roll in the shredded coconut, patting it into place with your hands to ensure it sticks. Freeze the cupcakes for at least 30 minutes, or until ready to serve.

Makes 12 cupcakes

1⅓ cups unbleached all-purpose flour

1 teaspoon baking powder

¼ teaspoon salt

4 tablespoons butter, softened

¾ cup granulated sugar

2 large eggs

¼ cup vegetable oil

½ cup buttermilk

1 teaspoon vanilla extract

FILLING

2 cups Rich Toasted Coconut frozen yogurt (page 40), slightly softened

VANILLA BUTTERCREAM FROSTING

1 cup (2 sticks) butter, softened

3 tablespoons milk

2 teaspoons vanilla extract

3–4 cups confectioners' sugar

3 cups sweetened shredded coconut

4 or 5 drops red food coloring (optional)

These cupcakes are like mini ice cream cakes — perfect for times when you want to treat yourself but don't want a whole layer cake in your freezer! The orange cupcakes are stuffed with my Creamsicle frozen yogurt and topped with an orange glaze. I recommend drizzling on the glaze shortly before serving. The filled cupcakes keep best in the freezer when they are unfrosted, so you can keep them on hand for any time a craving strikes and then just prepare the glaze quickly before serving.

1⅓ cups unbleached all-purpose flour

1 teaspoon baking powder

¼ teaspoon salt

4 tablespoons butter, softened

¾ cup granulated sugar

2 large eggs

¼ cup vegetable oil

2 teaspoons grated orange zest or ½ teaspoon orange extract

½ cup fresh orange juice

1 teaspoon vanilla extract

FILLING

2 cups Creamsicle frozen yogurt (page 33), slightly softened

ORANGE GLAZE

2 cups confectioners' sugar

3-4 tablespoons fresh orange juice

1 Preheat the oven to 350°F/180°C. Line a 12-cup muffin pan with paper liners.

2 Whisk together the flour, baking powder, and salt in a medium bowl.

3 Cream together the butter and granulated sugar in a large bowl until light and fluffy. Beat in the eggs, one at a time, followed by the oil.

4 Stir half of the dry ingredients into the egg mixture, followed by the orange zest, orange juice, and vanilla. Stir in the remaining dry ingredients, mixing just until no streaks of flour remain. Divide the batter evenly into the prepared muffin cups.

5 Bake for about 15 minutes, until a toothpick inserted into the center of each cupcake comes out clean and the top springs back when lightly pressed. Let the cupcakes cool completely on a wire rack.

6 When the cupcakes are cool, hollow them out using a cupcake corer or by using a paring knife to carefully remove a core of cupcake from the top. Reserve the top of each core to serve as a "plug" for the cupcake.

7 Fill each cored cupcake with 2 to 3 tablespoons of the frozen yogurt. Place the cake plug over the frozen yogurt to enclose it. Freeze for at least 15 minutes to allow the frozen yogurt to set up before glazing.

8 To make the glaze, whisk together the confectioners' sugar and orange juice in a medium bowl until smooth, then drizzle over the cupcakes. Serve immediately.

Makes 12

You can use a cupcake corer or a round cookie cutter that is about ½ inch in diameter to core your cupcakes. If you don't have one, use a small paring knife to cut a cone out of the center of the cake.

Baked Alaska is a combination of cake and ice cream covered in a mountain of meringue that is browned before serving. If you're looking for a showstopper, look no further than this easy-to-assemble recipe.

BROWNIE BASE

- ½ cup (1 stick) butter
- 4 ounces dark chocolate, finely chopped
- 1 cup sugar
- 2 large eggs
- ¼ teaspoon salt
- 1 teaspoon vanilla extract
- ⅔ cup unbleached all-purpose flour
- ½ cup chocolate chips

- 1 quart Vanilla Bean frozen yogurt (page 23), slightly softened

MERINGUE

- 8 large egg whites
- 1½ cups sugar
- ¼ cup water
- 1 teaspoon vanilla extract

1 Preheat the oven to 350°F/180°C. Lightly grease an 8- or 9-inch springform pan.

2 To make the brownie base, melt together the butter and chocolate in a small microwave-safe bowl in the microwave, in 30-second increments to avoid overcooking the mixture. Allow the mixture to cool slightly.

3 Whisk together the chocolate mixture and sugar in a large bowl. Beat in the eggs, one at a time, followed by the salt and vanilla. Whisk in the flour and stir until the flour is just incorporated and no streaks remain. Fold in the chocolate chips. Pour the batter into the prepared pan.

4 Bake for 30 to 35 minutes, until a toothpick inserted into the center comes out with only a few moist crumbs attached. Let the brownie base cool completely in the pan.

5 Remove the brownie base from the pan and place on a parchment paper–lined baking sheet or serving platter. Line an approximately 8-inch-diameter mixing bowl with plastic wrap and press the frozen yogurt into it to form a dome. Invert the bowl onto the brownie base and remove the bowl, leaving the plastic wrap in place on the frozen yogurt dome. Freeze until firm, at least 2 hours.

6 Just before serving, preheat the oven to 450°F/230°C or turn on the broiler.

7 To prepare the meringue, beat the egg whites in a large bowl until slightly foamy.

8 Combine the sugar and water in a small saucepan. Cook over medium-high heat until the sugar melts and comes to a boil.

9 As the sugar comes to a full boil, beat the egg whites until they reach soft peaks. Slowly drizzle the hot sugar syrup into the egg whites while mixing on medium speed, continuing until all the sugar syrup has been added. Add the vanilla. Continue to beat the meringue until it has cooled to room temperature, about 5 minutes.

10 Remove the plastic wrap from the frozen yogurt dome and spread the meringue into a thick layer over the frozen yogurt and brownie base using an offset spatula. When the dessert is completely covered, bake or broil for 3 to 5 minutes, until the meringue is golden on top. Alternatively, a kitchen torch may be used to brown the meringue. Serve immediately.

Serves 8

Unmold frozen ice cream onto brownie base.

Cover ice cream dome and base with meringue.

Toast meringue using a kitchen torch or the broiler.

A mudslide is a very adult concoction that features a combination of vodka, Kahlúa, and Irish cream liqueur. This variation features a coffee base and Kahlúa-laced whipped cream, all in a chocolate cookie crumb crust.

20 chocolate sandwich cookies, such as Oreos

4 tablespoons butter, melted

3 cups Dark Chocolate frozen yogurt (page 26), slightly softened

3 cups Coffee frozen yogurt (page 27), slightly softened

1 cup Chocolate Fudge Sauce (page 162)

1½ cups heavy cream

⅓ cup confectioners' sugar

¼ cup Kahlúa

1 teaspoon vanilla extract

1 Crush the cookies into fine crumbs in a food processor. Add the melted butter and process until the crumbs are thoroughly moistened. Pour the mixture into a 9-inch pie plate and press into an even layer over the bottom and sides of the pan. Freeze for at least 30 minutes, or until very firm.

2 Spoon the chocolate frozen yogurt into the crust and spread into an even layer. Spoon the coffee frozen yogurt on top of the chocolate layer, spreading it evenly. Freeze for at least 30 minutes, until the top of the pie is firm.

3 Warm the chocolate fudge sauce slightly in the microwave and pour over the top of the coffee frozen yogurt, spreading it into an even layer with a spatula. Freeze until very firm, 2 to 3 hours.

4 Beat the cream to soft peaks in a large bowl. Beat in the sugar, then fold in the Kahlúa and vanilla. Spoon the whipped cream onto the top of the pie. Serve immediately, or return to the freezer until ready to serve.

Serves 8–10

Peanut butter pie is a dessert that some people absolutely swear by, and once you've had a slice, it's not hard to see why. Peanut butter is one of those flavors that will get your mouth watering. When combined with a little bit of chocolate, it becomes downright addictive.

1 Pulse the cookies in a food processor until finely chopped. Add the melted butter and pulse to blend. Press the crumbs into the bottom of a 9-inch springform pan to make an even layer. Chill in the refrigerator until firm, at least 15 minutes.

2 Spread the frozen yogurt on top of the chocolate crust. Freeze until firm, about 30 minutes.

3 Soften the peanut butter by heating it in a small microwave-safe bowl in the microwave for 30 to 45 seconds. Spread on top of the peanut butter frozen yogurt, then freeze until firm, about 15 minutes.

4 Bring the cream to a simmer in a small saucepan. Pour over the chocolate in a small bowl and stir until the chocolate has completely melted and the mixture is smooth. Pour the mixture over the frozen peanut butter, gently spreading it into an even layer. Freeze until ready to serve.

Serves 8-10

24 chocolate sandwich cookies, such as Oreos

2 tablespoons butter, melted

1 batch Peanut Butter frozen yogurt (page 85), slightly softened

¾ cup crunchy peanut butter

½ cup heavy cream

5 ounces dark chocolate, finely chopped

PEANUT BUTTER CUP PIE

BUTTER PECAN PIE

Do you like pecan pie? This frozen twist on a holiday favorite just might give the classic recipe a run for its money. The filling of the pie is a butter pecan frozen yogurt, and it is topped with a layer of sticky caramel and crunchy toasted pecans.

1¼ cups graham cracker crumbs

¼ cup sugar

½ teaspoon ground cinnamon

¼ teaspoon salt

4 tablespoons butter, melted and cooled

1 batch Browned Butter Pecan frozen yogurt (page 90), slightly softened

1 cup Classic Caramel Sauce (page 164)

1 cup pecan halves, toasted

1 Preheat the oven to 350°F/180°C. Stir together the graham cracker crumbs, sugar, cinnamon, and salt in a large bowl. Pour in the melted butter and stir until the mixture resembles wet sand. Pour the mixture into a 9-inch pie plate and press into an even layer over the bottom and sides of the pan.

2 Bake the crust for 15 to 17 minutes, until firm. Let the crust cool completely.

3 Spoon the frozen yogurt into the cooled crust, spreading it into an even layer. Freeze for at least 15 minutes, until the top is firm.

4 Stir together the caramel sauce and pecan halves in a small bowl. Spread the mixture over the top of the pie. Freeze for at least 3 hours, or until ready to serve.

Serves 8-10

This isn't your average banana cream pie, which is typically made with vanilla pudding and banana slices. While it does have freshly sliced bananas on top of a vanilla wafer crust, the pie also has layers of caramel and uses my Roasted Banana & Salted Caramel frozen yogurt for the filling.

1¼ cups vanilla wafer cookie crumbs

2 tablespoons granulated sugar

4 tablespoons butter, melted and cooled

2 ripe bananas

1 cup Classic Caramel Sauce (page 164)

1 batch Roasted Banana & Salted Caramel frozen yogurt (page 48), slightly softened

1 cup heavy cream

⅓ cup confectioners' sugar

1 teaspoon vanilla extract

1 Combine the cookie crumbs, granulated sugar, and melted butter in a large bowl and stir until the crumbs are thoroughly moistened. Pour the crumbs into a 9-inch pie plate and press into an even layer over the bottom and sides of the pan. Freeze for at least 30 minutes, or until very firm.

2 Cut the bananas into ¼-inch-thick slices and arrange in a layer on top of the crust. Drizzle ½ cup of the caramel sauce over the banana slices.

3 Spoon the frozen yogurt into the crust, spreading it into an even layer. Freeze for at least 30 minutes, until the top of the pie is firm.

4 Beat the cream to soft peaks in a large bowl. Beat in the confectioners' sugar and vanilla until completely combined. Spoon the whipped cream onto the top of the pie. Freeze until the pie is very firm, at least 2 to 3 hours. Drizzle with the remaining ½ cup caramel sauce before serving.

Serves 8-10

If you're getting a little tired of serving up the same old pumpkin pie during the holidays, these individual pumpkin baked Alaskas might be just what the dessert doctor ordered. With a spicy gingersnap crust and a creamy pumpkin filling, they have all the right flavors. Plus, they can be prepared in advance, then finished with the meringue just before serving.

1 Lightly grease eight cavities of a 12-cup muffin pan.

2 Stir together the cookie crumbs, brown sugar, and ¼ teaspoon cinnamon in a large bowl until well combined. Add the melted butter and mix until the crumbs resemble wet sand. Press the crumb mixture into the base of the eight cavities of the prepared pan. Freeze until firm, at least 30 minutes.

3 Scoop out ¼-cup scoops of the frozen yogurt using a measuring cup and place each domed scoop on top of one of the frozen crusts in the muffin pan. Freeze until firm, at least 30 minutes or until ready to serve, then invert the pan to release the crusts.

4 Just before serving, preheat the oven to 450°F/230°C or turn on the broiler.

5 To prepare the meringue, beat the egg whites in a large bowl until slightly foamy.

6 Combine the granulated sugar and water in a small saucepan. Cook over medium-high heat until the sugar melts and comes to a boil.

7 As the sugar comes to a full boil, beat the egg whites until they reach soft peaks. Slowly drizzle the hot sugar syrup into the egg whites while mixing on medium speed, continuing until all the sugar syrup has been added. Add the vanilla and ½ teaspoon cinnamon. Continue to beat the meringue until it has cooled to room temperature, about 5 minutes.

8 Spread the meringue into a thick layer over the frozen yogurt and cookie base, using an offset spatula. When the dessert is completely covered, bake or broil for 3 to 5 minutes, until the meringue is golden on top. Alternatively, a kitchen torch may be used to brown the meringue. Serve immediately.

Serves 8

1 cup gingersnap cookie crumbs

2 tablespoons brown sugar

¼ teaspoon ground cinnamon

2 tablespoons butter, melted

2 cups Spiced Pumpkin Pie frozen yogurt (page 46), slightly softened

MERINGUE

8 large egg whites

1½ cups granulated sugar

¼ cup water

1 teaspoon vanilla extract

½ teaspoon ground cinnamon

SEMIFREDDOS, TERRINES, AND BOMBES

7

Semifreddo means "semifrozen" in Italian. These are dense, mousse-like frozen desserts made with unchurned frozen yogurt and served sliced rather than scooped. Frozen terrines are similar to semifreddos, as both are molded and sliced rather than scooped. They don't have the mousse-like texture of semifreddos and often combine different layers of flavor. Bombes are frozen yogurt desserts that are shaped in rounded molds using a mixing bowl or specialty mold.

This Neapolitan semifreddo offers something for everyone, all in one dessert. The layered treat is made with chocolate, strawberry, and plain frozen yogurts. While vanilla is more traditional for a Neapolitan dessert, the tangy plain yogurt provides a refreshing contrast to the rich chocolate and sweet berries. Serve each slice as is, or top with a drizzle of Easy Strawberry Sauce (page 166) or Chocolate Fudge Sauce (page 162) to play up your favorite flavors.

This dessert requires a deep springform pan. If your pan isn't deep enough to hold all three layers, make one layer separately and stack the layers together after everything is frozen.

1 batch Chocolate frozen yogurt (page 25), unchurned

1 batch Fresh Strawberry frozen yogurt (page 37), unchurned

1 batch Tangy & Tart frozen yogurt (page 22), unchurned

1 Line a deep 9-inch springform pan with plastic wrap. Pour the chocolate frozen yogurt into the pan and spread into an even layer. Freeze until firm, about 30 minutes.

2 Pour the strawberry frozen yogurt over the chocolate layer. Freeze until firm, about 30 minutes.

3 Pour the tangy frozen yogurt layer over the strawberry layer. Freeze for at least 3 hours before serving.

4 To serve, unmold the pan over a serving platter and peel off the plastic wrap. Cut with a hot, dry knife.

Serves 8-10

FUNFETTI SEMIFREDDO

This semifreddo was inspired by one of my favorite birthday cake styles: funfetti. Funfetti isn't a flavor as much as it is a style of cake. It is a vanilla cake base that has a generous quantity of rainbow sprinkles folded into it, creating a very colorful cake that is a festive dessert for any occasion. This frozen version includes both cake and sprinkles and is perfect for a party.

½ cup rainbow sprinkles

1 batch Vanilla Bean frozen yogurt (page 23), unchurned

1½ cups cubed pound cake (about one-quarter of a 9-inch loaf pound cake)

1 Line a 5- by 9-inch loaf pan with plastic wrap. Sprinkle about 2 tablespoons of the rainbow sprinkles evenly in the bottom of the pan.

2 Gently fold together the frozen yogurt and pound cake cubes in a large bowl. Quickly fold in the remaining 6 tablespoons rainbow sprinkles, making sure not to overmix the batter or allow the colors of the sprinkles to run. Pour the mixture into the prepared loaf pan. Tap the pan on the counter to release any air bubbles, then freeze until firm, at least 3 hours.

3 To serve, unmold the pan over a serving platter and peel off the plastic wrap. Cut with a hot, dry knife.

Serves 8–10

Spumoni is a molded, layered ice cream dessert with different fruits and nuts folded in. Most of us are most familiar with the commercial ice cream version that includes pistachio, cherry, and chocolate flavors. This frozen yogurt version is a delicious tribute to that classic! For the best results, I recommend adding a few drops of green food coloring to your pistachio frozen yogurt, as the dessert looks best with a little help from food coloring to capture the visuals that we associate with this dessert.

1 Line a 5- by 9-inch loaf pan with plastic wrap. Spoon the pistachio frozen yogurt into the pan, spreading it into an even layer. Freeze for 15 minutes.

2 Spoon the cherry frozen yogurt on top of the pistachio layer, spreading it into an even layer. Freeze for 15 minutes.

3 Spoon the chocolate frozen yogurt on top of the cherry layer, spreading it into an even layer. Freeze for at least 3 hours, or until ready to serve.

4 To serve, unmold onto a serving platter and peel off the plastic wrap. Cut with a hot, dry knife.

Serves 8-10

2½ cups Pistachio frozen yogurt (page 88), slightly softened

2½ cups Black Cherry Vanilla frozen yogurt (page 39), slightly softened

2½ cups Chocolate frozen yogurt (page 25), slightly softened

SPUMONI TERRINE

S'MORES ICEBOX TERRINE

S'mores lovers will enjoy this unusual twist on the classic campfire treat. Layers of fudge, marshmallows, and graham crackers capture all the elements you would typically find in a s'more, but with the addition of smooth, creamy vanilla frozen yogurt.

10–12 graham cracker squares

2 cups mini marshmallows

1 quart Vanilla Bean frozen yogurt (page 23), slightly softened

½ cup Chocolate Fudge Sauce (page 162), plus more for topping

1 Lightly grease a sheet of plastic wrap and line a 4- by 8-inch loaf pan with it.

2 Place a single layer of graham cracker squares on the bottom of the loaf pan, covering the entire base. Break some of the crackers to fit, if necessary.

3 Fold 1 cup of the mini marshmallows into the frozen yogurt. Spread 2 cups of the frozen yogurt mixture on top of the graham cracker layer, spreading it evenly.

4 Drizzle the fudge sauce over the top of the frozen yogurt layer, spreading it into an even layer. Place another single layer of graham crackers over the fudge sauce, again breaking to fit, if necessary.

5 Spread the remaining frozen yogurt into an even layer on top of the graham crackers. Cover with plastic wrap and press down firmly but gently.

6 Freeze for at least 2 hours, until very firm.

7 When ready to serve, unmold and remove the plastic wrap. Place the terrine smooth-side up on a serving dish. Warm some chocolate fudge sauce in the microwave, spread it on top of the terrine, and then top with the remaining 1 cup mini marshmallows. Lightly brown the mini marshmallows with a kitchen torch. (Or carefully put the terrine under the broiler for 1 minute — but do not do this if your frozen yogurt is very soft!)

8 Slice with a hot, dry knife and serve immediately.

Serves 8

Anyone who enjoys pumpkin pie should give this easy-to-make terrine a try during the holiday season. It's a great dessert to have ready in the freezer for when guests show up on short notice. Store the unchurned frozen yogurt in the fridge to keep it chilled as you layer this terrine.

1 batch Spiced Pumpkin Pie frozen yogurt (page 46), unchurned

1 batch Gingerbread frozen yogurt (page 73), unchurned

1 Lightly grease a 5- by 9-inch loaf pan, then line it with two layers of plastic wrap (a little oil will help the plastic wrap stick to the pan). Pour half of the pumpkin frozen yogurt into the pan and spread it evenly. Freeze for 30 minutes.

2 Pour half of the gingerbread frozen yogurt on top of the partially frozen pumpkin layer, spreading it evenly. Freeze for 30 minutes.

3 Pour the remaining pumpkin frozen yogurt on top of the gingerbread layer, spreading it evenly. Freeze for 30 minutes.

4 Pour the remaining gingerbread frozen yogurt into the pan, spreading it evenly. Cover the top of the pan with plastic wrap and freeze until very firm, at least 3 hours.

5 When ready to serve, turn the terrine out onto a serving plate and remove the plastic wrap. Allow to thaw at room temperature for 10 to 15 minutes, then cut it with a sharp, hot knife.

Serves 8–10

Red, white, and blue ice pops have been one of my Fourth of July staples since childhood. This bombe is inspired by those colorful pops and features stripes of red, white, and blue in each slice. Fresh berries add a very nice finishing touch before serving.

1 Line a 2½- to 3-quart bowl, preferably a ceramic, glass, or metal bowl, with two layers of plastic wrap and freeze for 10 to 15 minutes.

2 Spoon the strawberry frozen yogurt into the chilled bowl. Use the back of a spoon or a spatula to spread the yogurt into an even layer up the sides of the bowl, leaving a cavity in the center. Freeze for at least 30 minutes, or until firm.

3 Spoon the tangy frozen yogurt into the bowl on top of the frozen strawberry layer. Spread the yogurt into an even layer up the sides of the bowl. Freeze for at least 30 minutes, or until firm.

4 Spoon the blueberry frozen yogurt into the bowl on top of the tangy frozen yogurt. Pack the blueberry yogurt evenly to fill up the bowl, evening out the top. Freeze for at least 30 minutes, or until firm.

5 Remove the bombe from the freezer and invert onto a serving plate. If the bombe sticks in the bowl, place a warm, wet kitchen towel over the bottom of the bowl to help it release. Peel off the plastic wrap.

6 Beat the cream to stiff peaks in a large bowl. Beat in the sugar and vanilla. Spread the whipped cream over the top of the bombe and decorate with fresh berries. Freeze until ready to serve.

7 Cut the bombe into wedges with a hot, dry knife.

Serves 8

1 quart Fresh Strawberry frozen yogurt (page 37), slightly softened

1 quart Tangy & Tart frozen yogurt (page 22), slightly softened

2 cups Double Blueberry frozen yogurt (page 30), slightly softened

2 cups heavy cream

½ cup confectioners' sugar

1 teaspoon vanilla extract

Fresh blueberries and strawberries, for garnish

PIÑA COLADA BOMBE

You'll feel like you're on vacation just looking at this coconut-covered bombe. With layers of coconut and pineapple frozen yogurt, it delivers a taste of the tropics in every bite. Since it was inspired by a cocktail, this is finished off with a tasty rum sauce.

1 quart Roasted Pineapple frozen yogurt (page 50), slightly softened

1 quart Rich Toasted Coconut frozen yogurt (page 40), slightly softened

2 cups shredded sweetened coconut

2 tablespoons butter

½ cup firmly packed dark brown sugar

¼ teaspoon salt

6 tablespoons dark rum

1 Line a 2½- to 3-quart bowl, preferably a ceramic, glass, or metal bowl, with two layers of plastic wrap and freeze for 10 to 15 minutes.

2 Spoon the pineapple frozen yogurt into the chilled bowl. Use the back of a spoon or a spatula to spread the yogurt into an even layer up the sides of the bowl, leaving a cavity in the center. Freeze for at least 30 minutes, or until firm.

3 Spoon the coconut frozen yogurt into the cavity formed by the pineapple frozen yogurt, spreading it to even the top. Freeze for at least 30 minutes, or until firm.

4 Remove the bombe from the freezer and invert onto a serving plate. If the bombe sticks in the bowl, place a warm, wet kitchen towel over the bottom of the bowl to help it release. Peel off the plastic wrap.

5 Working quickly, press the shredded coconut against the sides of the bombe, covering it with a thin layer. Freeze for at least 30 minutes, or until firm.

6 Combine the butter, sugar, salt, and rum in a small saucepan. Bring to a boil, stirring until the sugar is dissolved, then cook the sauce until slightly thickened, 3 to 4 minutes. The sauce can be served hot or chilled.

7 When you are ready to serve the bombe, cut it into wedges with a hot, dry knife and drizzle each slice with rum sauce.

Serves 8–10

Step 2

Step 3

Step 4

Step 5

COOKIE LOVERS' BOMBE

You'll find two different types of cookie-laden frozen yogurt in this dessert: cookie dough and cookies 'n' cream. It's a dessert that will appeal both to the kid in you and to the grown-up with a sweet tooth.

10 medium chocolate chip cookies

1 quart Chocolate Chip Cookie Dough frozen yogurt (page 79), slightly softened

1 quart Cookies 'n' Cream frozen yogurt (page 76), slightly softened

20 chocolate sandwich cookies, such as Oreos

4 tablespoons butter, melted

1 Line a 2½- to 3-quart bowl, preferably a ceramic, glass, or metal bowl, with two layers of plastic wrap and freeze for 10 to 15 minutes. Place one chocolate chip cookie at the bottom of the bowl. Crush all of the remaining chocolate chip cookies into crumbs in a food processor.

2 Spoon the chocolate chip cookie dough frozen yogurt into the chilled bowl, forming a flat, even layer. Spread the chocolate chip cookie crumbs on top of the layer of cookie dough yogurt. Freeze for at least 30 minutes, or until firm.

3 Spoon the cookies 'n' cream frozen yogurt on top of the chocolate chip cookie crumb layer. Freeze for at least 30 minutes, or until firm.

4 Crush the sandwich cookies into fine crumbs in the food processor. Add the melted butter and process until the crumbs are thoroughly moistened. Pour the crumbs into the bowl on top of the frozen layer of cookies 'n' cream yogurt. Pack down gently to form a flat, even base. Freeze for at least 30 minutes, or until firm.

5 Remove the bombe from the freezer and invert onto a serving plate. If the bombe sticks in the bowl, place a warm, wet kitchen towel over the bottom of the bowl to help it release. Peel off the plastic wrap.

6 Cut the bombe into wedges with a hot, dry knife.

Serves 8

Chocolate and peanut butter always make a good combination, and it gets even better once you bring some bananas into the mix. Bananas seem to highlight the richness of chocolate while bringing out the savory side of peanut butter. Mini peanut butter cups are my favorite mix-in, but chopped-up regular-size peanut butter cups also work if you can't find the minis.

1 Line a 2½- to 3-quart bowl, preferably a ceramic, glass, or metal bowl, with two layers of plastic wrap and freeze for 10 to 15 minutes.

2 Spoon two-thirds of the chocolate frozen yogurt into the chilled bowl. Use the back of a spoon or a spatula to spread the yogurt into an even layer almost up to the top of the sides of the bowl, leaving a cavity in the center. Freeze for at least 30 minutes, or until firm.

3 Stir ½ cup of the peanut butter cups into the bananas Foster frozen yogurt and the remaining ½ cup peanut butter cups into the peanut butter frozen yogurt. Spoon the banana frozen yogurt into the chocolate yogurt shell, spreading it into an even layer. Spread the peanut butter yogurt on top of the banana yogurt, spreading it into an even layer. Freeze for at least 30 minutes, or until firm.

4 Spoon the remaining chocolate frozen yogurt into the bowl on top of the frozen peanut butter layer. Spread into a thin, even layer. Freeze for at least 30 minutes, or until firm.

5 Remove the bombe from the freezer and invert onto a metal cooling rack. Place the rack on a rimmed baking sheet. If the bombe sticks in the bowl, place a warm, wet kitchen towel over the bottom of the bowl to help it release. Peel off the plastic wrap. Pour the chocolate fudge sauce over the top of the bombe. Garnish with a handful of mini peanut butter cups. Freeze until ready to serve.

6 Cut the bombe into wedges with a hot, dry knife.

Serves 8

1 quart Chocolate frozen yogurt (page 25), slightly softened

1 cup mini peanut butter cups, plus more for garnish

2 cups Bananas Foster frozen yogurt (page 47), slightly softened

2 cups Peanut Butter frozen yogurt (page 85), slightly softened

1 cup Chocolate Fudge Sauce (page 162)

CHOCOLATE MALTED BOMBE

Slicing into this bombe won't quite deliver a classic soda fountain experience, but the flavors certainly will once they come together. The chocolate malt balls that serve as garnish for this bombe can be a little tricky to get into place, so make sure you reserve a little bit of ganache to act as extra "glue" when applying them.

1 quart Chocolate frozen yogurt (page 25), slightly softened

1 quart Chocolate Malted frozen yogurt (page 82), slightly softened

2 cups Fresh Strawberry frozen yogurt (page 37), slightly softened

1 cup heavy cream

10 ounces semisweet chocolate, finely chopped

4 cups chocolate malt balls

1 Line a 2½- to 3-quart bowl, preferably a ceramic, glass, or metal bowl, with two layers of plastic wrap and freeze for 10 to 15 minutes.

2 Spoon the chocolate frozen yogurt into the chilled bowl. Use the back of a spoon or a spatula to spread the yogurt into an even layer up the sides of the bowl, leaving a cavity in the center. Freeze for at least 30 minutes, or until firm.

3 Spoon the chocolate malted frozen yogurt into the bowl on top of the frozen chocolate layer. Spread the yogurt into an even layer up the sides of the bowl. Freeze for at least 30 minutes, or until firm.

4 Spoon the strawberry frozen yogurt into the bowl on top of the malted frozen yogurt. Pack the strawberry yogurt evenly to fill up the bowl, evening out the top. Freeze for at least 30 minutes, or until firm.

5 Bring the cream to a boil in a small saucepan. Pour the cream over the chocolate in a bowl and stir until the chocolate is melted. Allow the mixture to cool slightly, until it has thickened slightly but is still pourable.

6 Remove the bombe from the freezer and invert onto a metal cooling rack. Place the rack on a rimmed baking sheet. If the bombe sticks in the bowl, place a warm, wet kitchen towel over the bottom of the bowl to help it release. Peel off the plastic wrap. Pour the chocolate ganache over the top of the bombe. Working quickly, cover the chocolate ganache with the chocolate malt balls. If necessary, dip one side of the balls into leftover ganache to help them stick. Freeze until ready to serve.

7 Cut the bombe into wedges with a hot, dry knife.

Serves 8

POPSICLES, BONBONS, AND OTHER TREATS

8

Any frozen yogurt recipe can be made into popsicles or bonbons. For the popsicles, you can simply spoon the frozen yogurt into your molds just after churning. Since bonbons don't require a mold, it is better for the frozen yogurt to be a bit firmer before starting to shape them. All of these treats can be prepared in advance, so make some room in your freezer before starting out.

APPLE COBBLER POPS

Apple cobbler is often served warm, with a scoop of ice cream or frozen yogurt alongside it, but this easy frozen yogurt pop — an ode to the traditional dessert — really works.

2 cups Apple Pie frozen yogurt (page 43), freshly churned or slightly softened

1 cup crushed shortbread cookies

1 Fill eight ice pop molds almost halfway full with the frozen yogurt. Sprinkle 1 tablespoon of the crushed shortbread cookies into each mold. Fill the molds almost to the top with more frozen yogurt, then sprinkle an additional 1 tablespoon crushed cookies into each mold.

2 Place sticks into the pops and freeze until solid, at least 2 to 3 hours.

Makes 8 pops

A buttery cinnamon streusel runs through these frozen pops, adding a little bit of texture and a wonderful hint of spice. When you taste it combined with the browned butter in the frozen yogurt, you can't help but think of freshly baked cinnamon buns — and you might even be tempted to eat these for breakfast!

1 Whisk together the flour, oats, sugar, cinnamon, and salt until well blended. Add the melted butter, then stir with a fork until the mixture resembles wet sand and the butter is completely incorporated.

2 Pour the topping into a medium skillet and cook over medium heat, stirring frequently, until the mixture begins to brown, 3 to 4 minutes. When it starts to brown, stir slowly but constantly until the mixture is well toasted, 2 to 3 minutes. Transfer to a plate to cool.

3 Stir the cinnamon streusel into the frozen yogurt.

4 Fill eight ice pop molds almost to the top with the cinnamon streusel–swirled frozen yogurt.

5 Place sticks into the pops and freeze until solid, at least 2 to 3 hours.

Makes 8 pops

½ cup unbleached all-purpose flour

¼ cup quick-cooking oats

¼ cup firmly packed brown sugar

1 teaspoon ground cinnamon

⅛ teaspoon salt

4 tablespoons butter, melted and cooled

2 cups Vanilla Browned Butter frozen yogurt (page 61), freshly churned or slightly softened

KEY LIME PIE POPS

These pops almost couldn't be any easier to make, and for citrus fans like me, they couldn't be any easier to eat. The creamy, refreshing lime frozen yogurt is at its best when paired with a sprinkle of graham cracker crumbs to evoke the crust of a traditional Key lime pie.

2 cups Key Lime frozen yogurt (page 32), freshly churned or slightly softened

½ cup crushed graham crackers

1 Fill eight ice pop molds almost halfway full with the frozen yogurt. Sprinkle ½ tablespoon of the crushed graham crackers into each mold. Fill the molds almost to the top with more frozen yogurt, then sprinkle an additional ½ tablespoon crushed crackers into each mold.

2 Place sticks into the pops and freeze until solid, at least 2 to 3 hours.

Makes 8 pops

BLACK & WHITE CHOCOLATE POPS

These frozen yogurt pops are full of contrasts in colors and in flavors. Each pop has layers of both chocolate and vanilla frozen yogurt and is dipped in both dark and white chocolate. They are good even without the chocolate coating, but that finishing touch takes this treat from good to great.

1⅓ cups Dark Chocolate frozen yogurt (page 26), freshly churned or slightly softened

⅔ cup Chocolate Chip frozen yogurt (page 77), freshly churned or slightly softened

8 ounces white chocolate, finely chopped

5 ounces dark chocolate, finely chopped

1 Fill eight ice pop molds one-third full with the dark chocolate frozen yogurt. Add enough of the chocolate chip frozen yogurt to the molds to fill them two-thirds full. Top the molds off with the remaining dark chocolate frozen yogurt. If the freshly churned yogurt is overly soft and the layers begin to run together, freeze for 15 minutes between layers.

2 Place sticks into the pops and freeze until solid, at least 2 to 3 hours.

3 Melt the white chocolate in a microwave-safe bowl in the microwave in 45- to 60-second increments, stirring frequently, until the chocolate is completely melted and very smooth. Transfer the melted chocolate to a tall, narrow container. Unmold the pops and dip each into the white chocolate, allowing any excess to run off. Return the pops to the freezer for 15 minutes.

4 Melt the dark chocolate in a microwave-safe bowl in the microwave in 45- to 60-second increments, stirring frequently, until the chocolate is completely melted and very smooth. Transfer the melted chocolate to a narrow container and dip the top half of each pop into it, allowing any excess to run off. Return the pops to the freezer for at least 15 minutes before serving.

Makes 8 pops

These cute frozen lollipops are sure to get lots of oohs and aahs before they are eaten. You can make them in a variety of sizes and shapes, depending on what kind of cookie cutters you have on hand, though I recommend sticking to simple shapes for the best results. After dipping them in chocolate, scatter on some nuts, sprinkles, or coconut for a little variety!

1 Line a 9- by 13-inch pan with parchment paper. Pour the freshly churned frozen yogurt into the pan, then freeze until firm.

2 Line a baking sheet with parchment paper. Using a hot, dry metal cookie cutter (run the cookie cutter under hot water, then dry it quickly), cut the frozen yogurt into twelve 2½- to 3-inch rounds. Insert an ice pop or lollipop stick into each round. Set the rounds of frozen yogurt on the baking sheet and freeze until firm, at least 30 minutes.

3 Melt the chocolate in a microwave-safe bowl in the microwave in 45- to 60-second increments, stirring frequently, until the chocolate is completely melted and very smooth.

4 Working with one lollipop at a time, dip it quickly into the melted chocolate. Allow any excess chocolate to drain off, then sprinkle on any toppings, if using. Place the lollipop on the baking sheet and refreeze.

Makes 12 lollipops

1 batch frozen yogurt of your choice, freshly churned or slightly softened

8 ounces dark chocolate, finely chopped

Sprinkles, chopped nuts, chopped cacao nibs, toasted coconut, or chopped freeze-dried fruits, for topping (optional)

CHOCOLATE-DIPPED LOLLIPOPS

These bonbons are not only made with Nutella frozen yogurt, but they also have a core of chocolaty Nutella hiding inside. They can be a little messy to make if the centers aren't firmly frozen before you handle them, so take your time; your patience will really pay off. Try to keep the bonbons small, so that each one is just one or two bites, even though it may be tempting to make them larger.

¾ cup Nutella

1 cup chopped toasted hazelnuts

1 batch Nutella frozen yogurt (page 87)

8 ounces dark chocolate, finely chopped

1 Line a baking sheet with waxed or parchment paper. Scoop 32 teaspoon-size balls of the Nutella onto the paper and freeze until firm.

2 Spread the hazelnuts on a plate or baking sheet. Using a melon baller or small ice cream scoop, scoop the frozen yogurt into 1-inch balls, pushing one of the balls of frozen Nutella into the middle of each scoop with your finger. Roll the balls of frozen yogurt in the nuts, pressing gently to help them adhere. Place the bonbons on the baking sheet and freeze until firm, about 30 minutes.

3 Melt the chocolate in a microwave-safe bowl in the microwave in 45- to 60-second increments, stirring frequently, until the chocolate is completely melted and very smooth.

4 Working with one bonbon at a time, dip it into the chocolate using two forks, allowing the excess chocolate to run off. Return the bonbons to the freezer and freeze until ready to serve.

Makes about 32 bonbons

Salted caramels always get my mouth watering because of their sweet-salty notes. You'll get that same sensation in every bite of these bonbons!

1 Pour the freshly churned frozen yogurt into a 9- by 13-inch pan. Drizzle the caramel sauce over the frozen yogurt and sprinkle with the salt. Freeze until firm.

2 Using a melon baller or small ice cream scoop, scoop the caramel-topped frozen yogurt into 1-inch balls. Place the bonbons on a baking sheet and freeze until firm, about 30 minutes.

3 Melt the chocolate in a microwave-safe bowl in the microwave in 45- to 60-second increments, stirring frequently, until the chocolate is completely melted and very smooth.

4 Working with one bonbon at a time, dip it into the chocolate using two forks, allowing the excess chocolate to run off. Sprinkle the top of the bonbon with a few flakes of salt before returning it to the freezer. Freeze until ready to serve.

Makes about 32 bonbons

- 1 batch Dulce de Leche frozen yogurt (page 62), freshly churned
- ½ cup Classic Caramel Sauce (page 164)
- 1 teaspoon sea salt, plus more for sprinkling
- 8 ounces dark chocolate, finely chopped

This flavor combination was inspired by one of my favorite cookie combos: white chocolate and macadamia nut. The chopped macadamia nuts give the frozen bonbons a great texture that contrasts well with both the creamy white chocolate and the vanilla frozen yogurt.

1 batch Vanilla Bean frozen yogurt (page 23)

2 cups chopped toasted macadamia nuts

10 ounces white chocolate, finely chopped

1 Line a baking sheet with waxed or parchment paper. Using a melon baller or small ice cream scoop, scoop the frozen yogurt into 1-inch balls. Arrange the balls on the baking sheet and freeze until firm, at least 30 minutes.

2 Spread the macadamia nuts on a plate or baking sheet.

3 Melt the chocolate in a microwave-safe bowl in the microwave in 45- to 60-second increments, stirring frequently, until the chocolate is completely melted and very smooth.

4 Working with one bonbon at a time, dip it into the chocolate using two forks, allowing the excess chocolate to run off. Quickly roll each bonbon in the chopped nuts to coat, then return to the freezer and freeze until ready to serve.

Makes about 32 bonbons

Make sure your frozen yogurt is frozen solid before dipping each ball into the melted chocolate. Not only will this prevent the yogurt from melting, it will encourage the chocolate to harden quickly into an even layer.

PEANUT BUTTER & MILK CHOCOLATE BONBONS

To deliver peanut butter and milk chocolate in each bite of these bonbons, the two flavors of frozen yogurt are jumbled together — and then sprinkled with chopped-up peanut butter cup candies.

1 batch Peanut Butter frozen yogurt (page 85), slightly softened

1 batch Chocolate frozen yogurt (page 25), slightly softened

1 cup chopped chocolate peanut butter cups

10 ounces milk chocolate, finely chopped

½ cup chopped salted peanuts

1 Alternate scoops of the peanut butter and the chocolate frozen yogurts in a 9- by 13-inch pan. Sprinkle evenly with the chopped peanut butter cups and freeze until firm.

2 Using a melon baller or small ice cream scoop, scoop the frozen yogurt mixture into 1-inch balls, getting some chopped peanut butter cups in each scoop. Place the bonbons on a baking sheet and freeze until firm, about 30 minutes.

3 Melt the chocolate in a microwave-safe bowl in the microwave in 45- to 60-second increments, stirring frequently, until the chocolate is completely melted and very smooth.

4 Working with one bonbon at a time, dip it into the chocolate using two forks, allowing the excess chocolate to run off. Sprinkle the top of the bonbon with a few of the chopped peanuts before returning it to the freezer. Freeze until ready to serve.

Makes about 32 bonbons

Deep-fried ice cream is a decadent treat that we usually see only in restaurants or at county fairs. This un-fried version uses a sweet and crisp coating that is made on the stovetop, not in the deep fryer. It's easier to make than its counterpart, but it is just as delicious.

1 Spoon the frozen yogurt into eight ½-cup scoops, packing firmly to create balls, and arrange on a baking sheet or in the cups of a muffin pan. Freeze until firm, at least 1 hour.

2 Line a baking sheet with waxed or parchment paper. Melt the butter, sugar, and salt together in a medium saucepan over medium heat, stirring occasionally, until the sugar has melted and the mixture begins to boil. Boil for 1 minute, then stir in the cinnamon and cornflakes. Stir to coat the cornflakes, then remove from the heat and pour the mixture out onto the prepared baking sheet to cool. When cool, crush the cornflakes into fine crumbs and place in a large shallow bowl.

3 Take the frozen yogurt balls out of the freezer and roll in the cornflake crumbs, pressing the crumbs against the frozen yogurt to ensure that each scoop has an even coating. Freeze until firm, at least 30 minutes, or until ready to serve.

Makes 8 treats

1 quart Vanilla Bean frozen yogurt (page 23), slightly softened

4 tablespoons butter

½ cup sugar

¼ teaspoon salt

1½ teaspoons ground cinnamon

6 cups cornflakes

SUGAR COOKIE BOWLS

Instead of serving your frozen yogurt in a regular bowl, consider baking up a batch of these edible bowls. The buttery cookies are simple to make and are even more delicious than a traditional ice cream cone.

2¾ cups unbleached all-purpose flour

1 teaspoon salt

1 cup (2 sticks) butter, softened

1½ cups sugar

1 large egg

2 teaspoons vanilla extract

1 Whisk together the flour and salt in a medium bowl.

2 Cream together the butter and sugar in a large bowl until light and fluffy. Beat in the egg, followed by the vanilla. With the mixer on low speed, gradually blend in the flour mixture until the dough comes together. Divide the dough into two portions, wrap each in plastic wrap, and flatten into disks. Chill for at least 30 minutes.

3 Preheat the oven to 350°F/180°C. Turn a muffin pan upside down and grease the bottom of each cup.

4 Roll out the chilled dough on a lightly floured surface until it is about ⅛ inch thick. Use a 4½- or 5-inch round cutter (or a small bowl, along with a knife to cut around the edge, if you do not have a large enough cookie cutter) to cut rounds of dough. Drape the rounds over the upside-down muffin cups, pressing them gently into place. Repeat, gathering and rerolling the dough as necessary, until you have 12 rounds.

5 Bake for 12 to 14 minutes, until golden brown. Allow the cookie bowls to cool for about 10 minutes on the muffin pan, then transfer them to a wire rack to cool completely.

6 Store in an airtight container before filling with frozen yogurt and serving.

Makes 12 bowls

Carefully drape cookie dough over upside-down muffin cups to shape the bowls. Don't worry if the dough tears — just pinch it back together before baking.

156

CHOCOLATE-DIPPED COFFEE CREAM PUFFS

Cream puffs are handheld desserts that are just as much fun to make as they are to eat. These pack a coffee pick-me-up, as each pastry is stuffed with coffee frozen yogurt. I added a chocolate glaze to each of these puffs, and I highly recommend serving them with a dollop of whipped cream alongside.

CHOUX PASTRY

- ¼ cup milk
- ¼ cup water
- 3½ tablespoons butter, softened
- 1½ teaspoons sugar
- ½ teaspoon salt
- ¾ cup unbleached all-purpose flour
- 2 large eggs

CREAM PUFFS

- 1 batch Coffee frozen yogurt (page 27)
- ¾ cup chopped dark chocolate

1 Preheat the oven to 400°F/200°C. Line a baking sheet with parchment paper.

2 To make the choux pastry, combine the milk, water, butter, sugar, and salt in a small saucepan and bring to a boil over medium heat.

3 Add the flour all at once, stirring vigorously with a wooden spoon until the dough comes together into a ball. Continue to cook the dough, stirring continuously, for 1 minute.

4 Transfer the dough to an electric mixer with a paddle attachment and mix on low speed for 2 to 3 minutes, until the mixture has slightly cooled. Add the eggs one at a time, waiting until each egg is fully incorporated to add the next one. Increase the mixer speed and continue mixing until the batter is very smooth, 3 to 4 minutes.

5 Using a spoon, drop 16 rounded tablespoonfuls of the dough onto the prepared baking sheet.

6 Bake for 20 minutes, or until the puffs are well browned. Allow the puffs to cool completely on a wire rack.

7 Cut each cream puff almost in half. Scoop out a medium scoop of frozen yogurt and place inside the cream puff. Place on a baking sheet and freeze for 15 minutes.

8 Melt the chocolate in a small microwave-safe bowl in the microwave in 45- to 60-second increments, stirring frequently, until the chocolate is completely melted and very smooth. Dip the tops of the cream puffs in the chocolate, place them back on the baking sheet, and return to the freezer. Freeze until very firm.

Makes 16 cream puffs

9 SAUCES

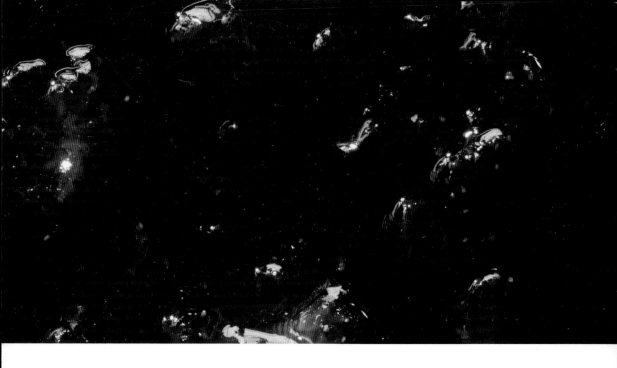

These toppings can be paired with just about every frozen yogurt flavor in this book — and you can also pair them with any store-bought frozen treats you might have in your freezer. I usually store mine in the refrigerator in mason jars, which are easy to open when I need a spoonful for my sundae (or my next snack).

CHOCOLATE FUDGE SAUCE

It's hard to go wrong with more chocolate when it comes to dessert. Fortunately, this velvety chocolate sauce will pair with just about any flavor of frozen yogurt that you can think of.

1 (14-ounce) can sweetened condensed milk

2 cups chocolate chips

¼ teaspoon salt

2 teaspoons vanilla extract

1 Combine the sweetened condensed milk, chocolate chips, and salt in a medium saucepan. Cook over medium heat, stirring frequently, until the chocolate has melted. Stir in the vanilla until the sauce is smooth, then remove from the heat.

2 Transfer the sauce to a storage container and let cool to room temperature, then cover and refrigerate until ready to use. The sauce will keep for at least 1 week. Reheat before serving.

Makes about 2 cups

You can always pick up a jar of caramel in the grocery store, but this sweet sauce is easy to make and much more delicious than the packaged varieties. A touch of salt and vanilla make this caramel sauce especially tasty.

½ cup sugar

¼ cup water

⅓ cup light corn syrup

¼ teaspoon salt

¾ cup heavy cream

1 teaspoon vanilla extract

1 Combine the sugar, water, corn syrup, and salt in a medium saucepan. Cook over medium heat, stirring with a spatula, until the sugar has dissolved. Once the sugar has dissolved, bring the mixture to a boil, then cook over medium heat until the mixture turns a rich amber color, 5 to 7 minutes. Pour in the cream. The mixture may bubble vigorously, but continue to cook it and stir with a spatula until the mixture has a uniform color and a smooth, creamy consistency. Remove from the heat and stir in the vanilla.

2 Transfer the sauce to a storage container and let cool to room temperature, then cover and refrigerate until ready to use. The sauce will keep for at least 1 week.

Makes about 1 cup

Bananas Foster is a dessert that dates back to the 1950s, when it was first served at Brennan's restaurant in New Orleans. Originally paired with vanilla ice cream, this rich banana caramel sauce is a great topping for almost any frozen yogurt flavor you can think of, vanilla included.

1 Halve the bananas lengthwise, then cut into ¼-inch-thick slices.

2 Combine the butter, sugar, and salt in a large skillet. Cook over medium heat, stirring frequently with a spatula, until the butter melts, the sugar dissolves, and the mixture begins to bubble. Allow the mixture to boil for 2 minutes, then stir in the bananas and cinnamon and cook until the bananas are tender, 2 to 3 minutes.

3 Turn the heat to low and carefully pour in the rum and vanilla. Simmer for about 2 minutes, then remove from the heat and serve warm.

Makes about 1½ cups

4 ripe bananas

5 tablespoons plus 1 teaspoon butter

½ cup firmly packed brown sugar

¼ teaspoon salt

½ teaspoon ground cinnamon

¼ cup dark rum

1 teaspoon vanilla extract

This sauce couldn't be any easier to make, and it will add both a pop of color and some berry sweetness to your frozen yogurt. You can use fresh berries when they're in season, but frozen berries are a great choice all year round.

1 cup fresh or frozen strawberries

¼ cup seedless strawberry jam

2 tablespoons sugar

2 teaspoons fresh lemon juice

1 Combine the strawberries, jam, sugar, and lemon juice in a medium microwave-safe bowl or in a small saucepan. If using the microwave, cook on high for 1 minute, then stir and cook for 60 to 90 seconds longer, until the sauce is bubbling and slightly thickened. If using the saucepan, cook over medium heat, stirring frequently, until the mixture comes to a boil and begins to thicken.

2 Allow the sauce to cool before serving or covering. The sauce can be stored in an airtight container in the refrigerator for up to 1 week.

NOTE: If you prefer a smoother sauce without chunks of berries, simply purée and strain the sauce to remove any solids.

Makes about 1 cup

You can use light or dark brown sugar to make this decadent homemade butter-scotch sauce. Light brown sugar will produce a golden color and a mild brown sugar flavor. Dark brown sugar will yield a deep amber color and a note of molasses. Both are good options, so it is worth making two batches to see which version will be your favorite!

4 tablespoons butter

½ cup firmly packed brown sugar

½ cup heavy cream

1 teaspoon vanilla extract

¼ teaspoon salt

1 Melt the butter in a medium saucepan. Add the sugar and cream. Bring to a boil, stirring to dissolve the sugar, and boil until the sauce has thickened and is smooth, 3 to 4 minutes. Stir regularly with a spatula or spoon as the mixture boils.

2 Remove from the heat and stir in the vanilla and salt.

3 Allow the sauce to cool before serving or covering. The sauce can be stored in an airtight container in the refrigerator for up to 1 week. Reheat before serving.

Makes about 1 cup

When you pour this chocolate sauce onto frozen yogurt, it forms a crisp chocolate shell as it cools. The effect seems like magic, but the secret to this sauce is coconut oil. Coconut oil turns hard more quickly and at higher temperatures than butter and some other fats.

1 Combine the chocolate and coconut oil in a medium microwave-safe bowl. Microwave in 30- to 40-second increments, stirring with a spatula in between, until the chocolate is completely melted and the mixture is smooth.

2 Drizzle or pour over frozen yogurt to serve. Leftovers can be stored in an airtight container in the refrigerator and reheated as necessary.

Makes about 1 cup

6 ounces semisweet or dark chocolate, finely chopped

2½ tablespoons coconut oil

METRIC CONVERSION CHARTS

Unless you have finely calibrated measuring equipment, conversions between US and metric measurements will be somewhat inexact. It's important to convert the measurements for all of the ingredients in a recipe to maintain the same proportions as the original.

WEIGHT

TO CONVERT	TO	MULTIPLY
ounces	grams	ounces by 28.35
pounds	grams	pounds by 453.5
pounds	kilograms	pounds by 0.45

US	METRIC
1 ounce	28 grams
4 ounces	112 grams
5 ounces	140 grams
8 ounces	228 grams
10 ounces	280 grams

VOLUME

TO CONVERT	TO	MULTIPLY
teaspoons	milliliters	teaspoons by 4.93
tablespoons	milliliters	tablespoons by 14.79
cups	milliliters	cups by 236.59
cups	liters	cups by 0.24
quarts	milliliters	quarts by 946.36
quarts	liters	quarts by 0.946

US	METRIC
1 teaspoon	5 milliliters
1 tablespoon	15 milliliters
¼ cup	60 milliliters
½ cup	120 milliliters
1 cup	230 milliliters
1¼ cups	300 milliliters
1½ cups	360 milliliters
2 cups	460 milliliters
2½ cups	600 milliliters
3 cups	700 milliliters
4 cups (1 quart)	0.95 liter
4 quarts (1 gallon)	3.8 liters

INDEX

Page numbers in *italic* indicate photos.

SAVOR SWEETNESS WITH MORE BOOKS FROM STOREY

by Megan Giller

This fascinating journey through America's craft chocolate revolution explains why a bar's flavor depends on where the cacao was grown; introduces some of today's hottest artisanal makers; and teaches how to successfully pair chocolate with coffee, beer, spirits, cheese, and bread.

by Brandi Scalise

Making scrumptious cookies has never been easier. With these 40 no-fuss recipes, just one bowl, and minimal baking equipment, you can whip up the ever-popular chewy chocolate chip cookie, the soon-to-be classic vanilla walnut pear cookie, and so much more.

by Valerie Peterson & Janice Fryer

Whether you want to decorate themed cookies for a baby shower, a birthday party, or a wedding, you'll find everything you need in this beautiful guide. Learn foolproof methods for rolling, baking, piping, flooding, and other key techniques.

by Laurey Masterton

More than 80 seasonal recipes, including Pork Tenderloin with Orange Blossom Honey-Mustard and Baked Acorn Squash, highlight eclectic honey varieties, such as sage and avocado. Soups, salads, main dishes, and desserts all radiate with the pleasures of nature's sweetener.

Join the conversation. Share your experience with this book, learn more about Storey Publishing's authors, and read original essays and book excerpts at storey.com. Look for our books wherever quality books are sold or call 800-441-5700.